# UnBrokable*

# III

## The 3rd 10 Reasons Why

### People Go Broke

## Despite Working

# Brad Kong

# Disclaimer

These are the full title and subtitle of this book:

***UnBrokable\* III:***
***The 3rd 10 Reasons Why** People Go **Broke Despite Working***

   I wrote *only* "***The 3rd 10 Reasons Why Broke***" on the front cover *intentionally* for rhyme, simplicity and focus.

   The graphic on this book cover is from Edit.org.  I use the site to design my covers; it provides book cover templates with its copy-righted images to writers who paid "annual memberships."

   I do have three proofs of my membership to Edit.org, payment receipt for the membership through Paypal and reference address to the image of the site.  I am writing this because I received emails regarding my "book cover images" twice; both of which were resolved within a day.  I decided to stick to my own or edit.org's images since I cannot keep getting copyright emails.  If you have any issue regarding my cover art, feel free to contact me: I will be more than happy to provide the three proofs again.

# Also by Brad Kong

**UnBrokable\* series:**

*Introduction to UnBrokable\**
*UnBrokable\* I* (Chapter 1 to 10)
*UnBrokable\* II* (Chapter 11 to 20)

**UnBrokable\* Sketch series:**

*Introduction to UnBrokable\** (Chapter 1 to 5)
*Intro to UnBrokable\* Large Print*

*UnBrokable\* I* (Chapter 1 to 10)
*UnBrokable\* II* (Chapter 11 to 20)
*UnBrokable\* III* (Chapter 21 to 30)
*UnBrokable\* IV* (Chapter 31 to 40)
*UnBrokable\* V* (Chapter 41 to 50)
*UnBrokable\* VI* (Chapter 51 to 60)
*UnBrokable\* VII* (Chapter 61 to 70)
*UnBrokable\* VIII* (Chapter 71 to 80)

*UnBrokable\** (Chapter 1 to 80)

**Brad Short Story Collection I:**

*Robbery at Cyb Knight*
*How to Get Rid of Ladies*
*11 Girls I had Loved*
*Say No To TSLA*
*3 Ways to Avoid Divorce*
*15 Ways to Keep Your Teeth Healthy*
*5 Moments When I Felt Sorry For My Cat*
*Corn Dog Grandpas*

*Condo Chronicle*
*How to Lose 40 Pounds*

**Brad Short Story Collection II:**

*15 Things You Didn't Know About Korea*
*3 Reasons Why We Need to Buy a Home Early*
*Why Are CDs Super Important?*
*Say No To TSLA (2nd Edition)*
*Large Pizza for $5*
*30 Reasons Why I am Great*
*3 Reasons Why the Nursing Home filed Bankruptcy*

# Praise for *UnBrokable*

"This is the best book I have ever read.  I am saying this only because Brad is my husband."

-Tsina D,
A housewife and teacher

"I cannot believe my dad wrote this much thick book.  He must be a genius."

-Yuna K,
An elementary school student

"I am proud of my son who wrote a book in English."

-Mrs. Jin,
A wealthy woman

"Publishing this book is a celebration itself.  Write your name on the next page if you bought this for a gift."

-Brad K,
A philosopher, writer, publisher, book designer and investor

# Un*Brokable*\*

Dear _____

This book is my gift for you.
It has been helpful for me, so I hope it will be
helpful for you as well.
Thank you always.
Sincerely,

From _____

For All the Honest Workers
Struggling Everyday

# Foreword

So many books out there from Self-Help and Financial Gurus talk about personal finances in abstract terms. These are folks who make millions selling books telling us what to do. Here is something new and refreshing, however. The author relates his real-life experiences in personal finance. Not only is there a lot of good advice in here, it is an interesting look into someone else's life.

It seems we are at a time in history where everyone is struggling to get ahead. But then again, if we look back in history, it has always been this way. The inflation of today pales to that of the 1970's. The unemployment of a few years ago was nothing like that era, either. What is frustrating for so many is that even "making good money" people are living "paycheck to paycheck" and wondering where the money all went. I know I fell into this trap!

The author illustrates how people go broke even while making a hefty salary, and provides a guide to being "UnBrokable" - a term he has coined. And apparently it works - he retired at 40, not from selling self-help books (like so many Gurus do) but by being careful with money.

There is a lot here to learn from. And it's only just getting started!


**Robert P. Bell**
Georgia
USA


Mr. Robert P. Bell is a retired Patent Attorney, self-made millionaire and founder of the popular blog named Living stingy (http://livingstingy.blogspot.com).   He has written in the last 15 years since 2008 and helped tons of people get out of debts and money problems.  He is well known for his humorous witty but sharp writing style and has influenced myriads of writers and bloggers including Brad Kong.

# Contents

## UnBrokable* II

## UnBrokable* III

## UnBrokable* IV

## UnBrokable* VII

67. Not Solving Housing Problem Quickly

68. Much on Ceremonies & Anniversaries

69. Not Using Infrastructure Already Built

70. Not Working While Being Wealthy

## UnBrokable* VIII

71. Going Too Big

72. Not Being Awake

73. Too Fantasizing Wealth

74. No Long Term Vision

75. Being Deceptive

76. Being On the Wrong Side

77. Not Going Straight to "Profitable or Not"

78. Having Low Self Esteem

79. Not Being Constructive

80. Not Having Enough Room to Breathe

Epilogue

Quotes by Brad

About Brad

# Prologue

*Dying poor is a shame, especially in wealthy countries.*
*It is not about money; it shows how we have lived.*
-Brad Kong

This is me sitting on the Ferrari in Miami, FL in 2003. Then, I didn't
expect I would go abysmally broke and suffer for long. I had to work
as a weekend dishwasher for 7 years from 2015.

Jack Whittaker was a construction businessman in
Putnam County, WV; he was known as the winner of a
lottery jackpot of $315 million in the Powerball in 2002.
He was a millionaire already with a net worth of $17 M
before winning – in a word, a rich man won a huge
lottery.

Oddly, a series of unfortunate events started happening to him afterward. First, a guy named Tribble, the boyfriend of Whittaker's granddaughter Brandi, was found dead from drug overdose in Whittaker's home in September, 2004; three months later, Brandi herself was also found dead at the age of 17; it shows that cocaine and methadone were found in her body. Five years later, Bragg, who was the mother of Brandi and Whittaker's daughter, was also found dead in Daniels, WV; the police suspected OD again. Then, Whittaker's home in Bland County, VA, was reported to be on fire in 2016. Finally, Mr. Whittaker himself passed away following a long illness at the age of 72 in 2020: *Why did the luckiest guy in the world pass away relatively early after losing all his children?*

Han Liu was a Chinese billionaire, the former chairman of Hanlong Group known for mining businesses. His assets were claimed at $6 billion USD by the time he passed away at the age of 49 in 2015. He was convicted of murdering 8 people and running a mafia-style gang for his businesses; he was executed by the law enforcement in China. His last words had been viral: "Life is short; *we don't have to live too diligently for more money.* I will have a small shop next life and live happily with my family."

The episodes above gave me a lesson: we don't have to work to death, make a lot, spend more and leave a fortune to others; I do not want to *grind* myself to donate more. In *Psychology of money* by Housel, there is a story of a man named Read; he was a janitor for 42 years, made a fortune out of blue-chip stocks, left $8 million to a hospital and passed away.  I know a similar case of Groner who worked as a secretary for 43 years, made profit out of the Abbott shares, left $7 million to a local college and died.  They were undoubtedly honorable.  But, seriously, *what's the point?*  What would be the thing they regretted the most?  As long as I have enough, **I conclude that the best reward I can give to myself is *working less.*** I may not need a luxury car, but I like to save myself from being offended.

Have you ever been a dishwasher before?  **If you don't fully agree with this book, it's possible you might not have been broke enough.**  I believe a guaranteed way to stay *sufficient* is staying away from the reasons causing poverty.  Coincidentally, I was in Chinatown Chicago the other day; it had some Korean shops, which were crowded.  It took forever for Korea to be wealthy.  Ironically, once people become rich, I learned  they can make money out of it: *Being rich itself can be a source of income.*

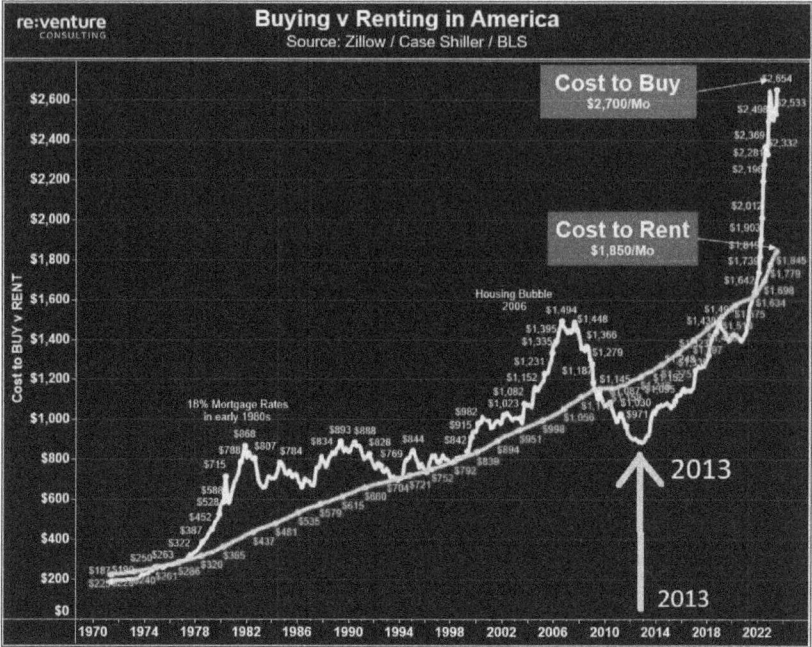

re:venture CONSULTING — **Buying v Renting in America**
Source: Zillow / Case Shiller / BLS

Cost to Buy $2,700/Mo

Cost to Rent $1,850/Mo

Housing Bubble 2006

18% Mortgage Rates in early 1980s

2013

2013

I bought my home in November, 2013. I didn't know it was the lowest price ever in the 21st century (source from Zillow).

My net worth has increased 8 times in the past decade. I had $80,000 CDs in the bank in 2013: How do I recall it? I bought my condo at full price of $60,000[1] that year; my real estate agent asked me to submit proof of funds in advance; I didn't know what to do, so I got a receipt from the ATM and gave it to her. Now I have over a $650,000 portfolio, not including my residence, as of 2023. This growth has probably been from inheritance, investment success, salaries and frugality. But I would say that "not having rent or mortgages" played a crucial role.

---

[1] It was low due to the economic depression then.

I enjoyed my life until I couldn't. And some of us may not since a recession may approach sooner or later. Maybe this book is not for the super-rich, the middle-class or even mildly poor. I had been in deep trouble myself, especially around 2009. My business wasn't doing well; the subprime mortgage crisis broke out; my car was a decade old; horrible mechanics kept overcharging me amid despair; then my daughter was born in 2010. I couldn't waste even a single cent for long, but I was able to manage to buy a small condo thanks to my parents; the only advantage was all the housing prices collapsed due to foreclosures during the heavy depression. This book is about *suffering less* for those: **Unlucky people who have no idea how to get out of poverty.** The Ferrari photo was taken 20 years ago in 2003; then, I had no idea how much trouble I was about to go through. Now I know that being wealthy is a combination of skills, knowledge and *luck*. On the contrary, being broke can happen any time on no significant grounds.

* * *

Charles Bukowski (1920 – 1994) was an American poet considered "the laureate of low-life" in the 1970s; he bought his first house 23 years *slower* than me. His net worth was over $4 million by the time he passed away: How did that happen? Mr. Bukowski was often considered a drunk loser, but I found out that he and I share a few things in common. First of all, we both started writing careers after our 40s; both had or have one daughter. We both had worked for low income physical

21

jobs; we both inherited some money from parents after becoming middle aged men.  Also both were born in foreign countries, originally.  But it shows that *Buk* bought his first house with a mortgage at the age of 58 in 1979; I bought my condo with cash at the age of 40 in 2013.  It took an extra 5 years for him to pay off his mortgage (which was fast).  As a result, he ended up buying his house 23 years later than me: What made him delay this long?

It is natural if someone goes broke when he or she does not have a job.  But some live poor even though they work full-time.  More ironically, some live wealthy without having a job: *How?*  For instance, my mother was initially from a poor family (typical old Koreans) and never had a real job.  But she has been in the top income class in the country for most of her life: What happened?  Again, let me start this 2nd edition of *UnBrokable\* III* by congratulating you – picking up this book means, at least, one step closer to wealth.  This series will be a practical and unorthodox guide to stay away from *brokeness*; we will talk about unique reasons, examples and facts, which can be my memoir, too.  **Brokeness (not brokenness[2]) is a noun** meaning **"the characteristic of not having enough money."**

Have you ever been broke before even though you have a job?  Have you been short of money despite working full-time?  People may not get broke automatically, especially in wealthy countries; if some are poor despite

---

[2] *Brokenness* means "a condition in which something is badly damaged."

working to death, I think there must be reasons. *What would you believe makes a person poor? Why do some still rent an apartment after working 12 hours a day for 30 years?* I had witnessed a couple of those closely for 7 years. *UnBrokable** may not be a word we can find in a dictionary yet as I coined it: **A person who cannot be financially broke is *UnBrokable*;** the opposite of *Les Miserable*. I think that there is a big misconception in our lives: If we work hard, we will be rich. Nothing can be further from the truth; *in fact, working longer can make us poorer;* some live painfully by exploiting themselves that way.

This book is a collection of my own survival stories in a sense; I am a middle-aged man with a wife and daughter from the Midwest. I think my American life can be divided into four periods since 1999.

1. Colleges: Cornell and SUNY at Buffalo (1999-2005)
2. Business: Cyb Knight Video Games (2006-2014)
3. Employment: A nursing home (2015-2022)
4. Investor and writer (2022 - current)

Or I can divide the 24 years by jobs:

- College banquet (2001 - 2002)
- eBay seller (2003 - 2015)
- Cyb Knight store Owner (2006-2014)
- Nursing home dishwasher (2015-2022)
- Investor and writer (2011-current)

There are other jobs with licenses I prefer not to mention now (pharmacy technician and medical coder). Also I have worked for myriads of small jobs since high school: convenience store clerk, bar kitchen helper, military soldier, etc.

* * *

Out of all those jobs, the recent *weekend dishwasher* gave me the inspiration to write *UnBrokable\** series. The nursing home I worked at is within walking distance from my home. I had a chance to volunteer to work one day in 2015; unexpectedly, it brought me a permanent weekend position. Then, I had not done anything for a year after closing out my video game store permanently in 2014. At the end of the work, they suddenly wondered (literally begged) if I could do the job at least every weekend. Now I see the reason why as I asked similar questions to other temp workers myself. For some reason, those nursing homes always need employees while no one is excited to labor there. Since they suggested a reasonable pay and plenty of free food from the kitchens, I accepted their offer. I had the job only on weekends for six years and on Sunday for a year, which was close to seven years in total.

I never liked that job since it was physically hard, but I have to admit that it has been helpful for my life. First, I had chances to meet a lot of people I would have not without it; there are types of people doing dishwashing for life. Nothing wrong, but I think I was able to see some reasons why they got stuck there: **The reasons for**

**keeping them in chains.** I think I had good chances to take a look at their lives; some were *truly great* guys, though. Secondly, the job had brought me physical strength; I have lost a lot of weight, especially in the beginning and gained muscles continuously. Thirdly, these weekend extra salaries, bonus and free food still helped me build up my savings faster.

There could be millions of reasons why people go broke: gambling, drug addictions, car accidents, etc; we cannot help those getting in obvious troubles. **Nonetheless, there are millions apparently not doing anything wrong, but always being broke while working**; many have nothing left in their accounts after some payments at the end of month.

* * *

Do you know when I had the hardest time with money? While I worked at the video game store, my daughter was born in 2010. When a baby is born, parents need more money while physically exhausted to take care of the baby. Incidentally, the mortgage bubble burst in 2008 and severe depression came from 2009: The *subprime mortgage crisis*. I guess that businesses must have a hard time these days as COVID has been with us since 2020; the impact may not be over soon. While I had wasted a massive amount of my parents' money only to keep my store open, the only good thing I did was buying a condo in full. Since the economy collapsed in 2008, there had been plenty of foreclosures, short sales and discounted houses on the market – getting rid of my rent and mortgage for good was the only upside during that era.

After having difficulty with money myself and watching others struggling, I started wondering what really makes a laborer in trouble: **Is there any *practical trap* to make full-timers broke even in wealthy countries?** While working in the nursing home, I saw dishwashers still renting apartments even after *30* years of employment. They occasionally worked *double*, which means up to 15 hours a day: Where did all their money go?

Are you ready to jump into 80 chapters with thousands of examples? **All the episodes are either from my life or true events throughout history.** I wonder if this will be the longest series you've finished since you cannot put it down. By the time we reach the epilogue, I hope that we will be more mature, knowledgeable and a bit closer to wealth.

# 21

# Approaching too Many Women

*Love is gone; it left me my wife and daughter.*
-Brad Kong

Did you know that the legendary womanizer Giacomo
Casanova had been in prison for 14 months for a sexual
charge[3] and almost went to jail a few times more for debt[4]?
He was a prodigy by birth and made a fortune from being
the state lottery salesman in France, but virtually had
spent all on women.  Pennilessly, he died of syphilis in
Duchcov Castle, Czech Republic in 1798.  I guess **being
obsessed with women and saving money didn't go
well together.**  A buddhist monk Pomnyun once said
that there is no desire lasting *forever*.  I think it's
particularly true for women.  Have you seen a photo of the
celebrity you used to like a decade ago?  Aging is a more
sensitive issue for ladies since people tend to care less
about men's appearances.  We can get attracted to anyone.
But, if this is not it, I think we should let the person go.

---

[3] He was originally sentenced to 5 years.
[4] It had been common to go to prison because of financial debt in Europe
even decades ago.

Weirdly, I believe having sex can be actually labor: A painful homework assigned by nature.  In my opinion, there are only two types of men chasing women after becoming 50: the greedy and the stupid.  Having fine relationships with women is not chasing – stalking is approaching women too much until they, including people around, feel uncomfortable.  **Wise men already know that there is no fantastic woman existing**; they already know that there is no real difference between men and women in privacy.  Therefore, there is no need to desire someone desperately, especially if we have had a marriage before – at least, not up to the point that it can cause trouble or a financial loss.

**We feel there are remarkable beauties somewhere only because women try so hard to be like one.**  For example, I don't remember the last time I heard my wife fart or saw her go to the bathroom to poop: Why?  I think she's holding it when I am at home – trying so hard to be a terrific girl.  I assume this is why she gets upset if I stay in the house too long, sometimes.  Some women spend hours to have make-up on, or weeks going through plastic surgeries and aftercare.  If we know what's going on behind doors, there is *absolutely* no reason to be eager for a specific one.  Mature men know this from diverse experiences, including marriage, childbirth or caring, by the time they become middle-aged.

On the contrary, **idiotic greedy men address every woman;** some go for physical instincts no matter what.  There was an old fat Mexican in the nursing home where I used to work; Pancho had been a dishwasher for 35 years, but didn't even own a house even though he was 60; he had rented a two-bedroom townhouse for $1,200 a month for decades then. He had three adult children[5] and two grandkids; probably seven people, including his wife, had lived together. Despite his misfortune, everyone didn't really like him much; I found him sneaky and selfish when doing jobs. He was particularly notorious for approaching young girls (usually servers), regardless of others' eyes; he had a bad reputation for having flirtations with touching in the middle of public.

There was a Mexican girl with fat butt named Ari[6]. I witnessed that some girls, especially Latinas at the nursing home, had a lot of flirtings with old men. To me, **these girls were equally disgusting or even worse than old men** (she was, at least). Think about it – what can those old men really lose? Nothing – they may get free intercourses if they are "lucky." On the other hand, these young girls do not gain anything out of it; they only get a tainted reputation repelling boys around. What Ari (20 then) did was keep looking for Pancho although everyone knew he was married. Even his daughter was working there as well, but they didn't seem to care, which was disrespectful for her. Those two made me uncomfortable until I resigned that job by 2022.

\* \* \*

---

[5] Unfortunately, his adult son passed away by an accident in 2019.
[6] Her father is Mexican and mother is white.

**Is getting married *profitable* in a financial sense?** By the time my daughter was born, I heard the following from the radio by chance: "The typical middle-aged married man has three times more assets than his unmarried peers – if we are married and stay in marriage, we will end up being more opulent than a single." It was brief, but an eye opening for me.

I had never been interested in marriage before hearing it although I have been married all along since 2010[7]. I had always considered a wedding and marriage as extra spendings, which is true in countless cases – nothing but a ceremony some adults go through? Nonetheless, can it really be a money generating tool for men? I did some research on it continually and concluded that it is not true. And here is the real reason I assume why a married man can end up being wealthier: **Women choose men with better futures, to begin with**; women select richer men from the start. Or women will choose men who they believe may make more money later on.

Before blaming all the women as gold diggers, let me give you a comparison. Suppose someone said, "Married women tend to be thinner than single women in their 40s": Does this mean a marriage makes a woman lose weight? No. More likely, men choose skinnier women to date from the beginning; at least, men never choose a super obese as a partner; overweights can stay single that way. In a word, all the married men passed some sorts of tests by women these days; the top priority is self

---

[7] I met my wife in 1999.

supporting capability of men. **I do not think marriage itself makes a man wealthier.** In fact, it brings men more expenses, especially after having children. I like to reassure that approaching more women will never be profitable – better not to go crazy about it.

\* \* \*

I felt Pancho above made his life that way; I don't think the wage those dishwashers get paid was that significantly small, especially working double shifts like him, virtually everyday. For the comparison, another dishwasher Omar, a Mexican boy living at his parents' home, had saved over $80,000 after working there for 8 years. I bought my condo 10 years ago even though I am much younger than Pancho; since condo association fees are four times smaller than rents in my neighborhood, it seems **he actually gets poorer every month.** If he gets another child after approaching other women persistently, he won't be out of poverty for good. Obviously, dishwashing is a hard job to endure for hours without having a bit of fun. Still, I think he should have changed his job rather than keep flirting out of boredom. There are a myriad of jobs paying more than dishwashers, anyway.

Today, I read in *The Wall Street Journal* that Tesla founder Musk had committed adultery with the ex-wife of the Google CEO, Brin and it caused the divorce of Brin's family; the ex-wife's name was Shanahan, who was a Chinese descendent. This was honestly stupid and disgusting. I will never buy a Tesla car or stock since I don't want to support dishonor.  Besides, I believe *wrongdoing brings profit loss to a corporation for one way or another*.  Regardless, I have to confess that I didn't like the face of the ex-wife looking like a gold digger having plastic surgeries.  She peculiarly reminds me of the Korean singer Park in chapter 8, who also had suspicions of having adultery with a married IT CEO in Korea back in 2019.  I don't know why, but both women look similar and necessarily chose married men who already had two kids respectively; Jo, the Korean IT CEO, had two kids before meeting Park; Brin had two children before meeting Shanahan as well, which is a bizarre coincidence.

I understand that Musk may have some money, but I don't think any man wants to be in his shoes: Wiki shows that he divorced three times and has *ten* kids by 2023.  No man wants to be in that kind of trouble requiring gigantic responsibilities.  I am sure I will not enjoy changing one more diaper or spending money on someone else doing so.  Frankly, I think men get the maximum happiness when they become *half-monks* after marriage; I am not saying that we need to be a Buddha.  I mean our lives tend to get much easier when we let go of some desires, including physical ones.  Unexpectedly, I found it's not that super hard as I get old, which was unimaginable in my 20s.

I conclude that I would have gotten fed up with whoever I get married to by now; I would have felt bored after seeing the same person for decades and it does not matter whoever it is.  It does not mean I hate my wife, but I am sure I won't get excited forever.  Quite frankly, we do not have to get married, from the start – being single is a legitimately great option. On the contrary, it just costs a lot if something goes wrong after marriage. It is ok not to have a lot of dating or partners; sometimes, unnecessary pressures are from our own DNAs; we will get happier when we relieve those somehow; maybe giving birth to a child once or having religions can help. Still, I think there are things we would better not do even if we want it badly.

There was a two story house I badly wanted in Roselle, IL in 2012; I remember I woke up in the middle of the night; I wanted it so bad that it was in my dream. I am truly glad I did not go for that then when I think about it now. The house is in a poor Mexican neighborhood known to have occasional blackouts from storms. Roselle has the smallest, yet poorest library in Chicagoland, despite its high property tax, and it is not even close to that house – my current condo is like 500 times better, when I see it now.

* * *

Sometimes, a perfectly smart man makes irrevocable mistakes only because of women – I think humans are built that way. Maybe those unreasonable actions caused by sexual desire is how the human race has survived for millions of years. Some think having high standards for partners is a bad thing; a few complain that, "I don't feel any girl is pretty enough for me anymore." This happens especially more to those watching too much media full of beautiful women.  Ironically, I don't think this is a really bad thing; in fact, the other way around is worse.

If a man has a too high standard, I don't think he will be deceived by gold diggers easily.  He can literally turn himself into a *Zen master* overcoming all the desires without practicing.  Since no girl is good enough, he can make a rational choice among those "*average*" looking females when he gets married.  Chasing too many women is a bad thing; these tend to have low standards.  **Getting disappointed by so-so looking girls will never cause trouble.**  In real life, there are men who think every woman is good enough and try to take every single opportunity; they are the ones who will get AIDS; they may make their wives upset; they will stay badly off for life.

**I think having too much sexual desire is a curse**, particularly for men.  Some men, especially singles who were raised without a sister, think there are super sophisticated mysteries about women; they are just being idiotic.  It took almost fifty years for me to master this concept thoroughly: "Women are like men." Men will naturally learn it when they have a wife and daughter for more than a decade like me; without them, I might have still thought women are mythical creatures, which is unrealistic.  This fantasy will not help us much in reality, particularly when we have to choose a partner. We all know that getting involved with a wrong woman costs a lot or even a life in some cases.

* * *

Personally, I just don't see a worse *"real life"* example than Pancho at the nursing home. I liked most Mexicans there in general, but everyone did not like him; he was a traitor on sharing jobs and gave me a headache until the last day I worked. I witnessed that he frequently worked 15 hours a day throughout the seven years; more correctly, he had stayed 15 hours a day at work while assigning his job to others in a sneaky way. He was not frugal – He was purely poor. He said that he had spent a total of $1,800 a month including rent, utilities, cell phones, etc for his whole family (six people). His adult daughter was working there as well. It's queer since **a few dishwashers even own a three-bedroom house in full.**

One thing I noticed was he approached women excessively – this guy never missed a chance to eat something tasty in the kitchen or talk to a girl. By nature of their business, nursing homes have plenty of female coworkers all the time: servers, dining managers, CNAs, nurses, cleaners, etc. His raider had been always on for women and an addressing plan started as soon as he detected one. He did it in a slow, but obvious and disgusting manner – friendly talk with females out of nowhere. His attitude changed quickly to be hostile towards male workers if he needed to talk to one. He had a horrible reputation since he helped only women while checking any advantage to take. *This was the reason why he had been dirt poor despite working.*

He approached a lot of young girls, too: **What is the point even if I get married to a new young lass again?** I do not want to waste my life wondering if she was married to me because of my money; I do not want to live in suspicion that she may meet another stallion for sex. Home should be the most comfortable place in the world: I do not want to break my nerves or create distress in my own place. Men are not cautious about women instinctively; they think women are weak and safe creatures. In real life, a lot of chicks are heavier, stronger or even taller than me. If not, still men can go down because of weaker ones; a known example is the musical *Carmen*. Including Trump, I would say only stupid men are getting married more than once.

* * *

There are three types of women I strongly recommend for men not to get close to.

1. Smokers and drinkers
2. Women having plastic surgery, including a tattoo
3. Women with no solid income.

There was a Jazzercise business next door when I had the video game shop; it moved in, 6 years after I opened my store. Three women owned it and they all pretended they made a lot of money – especially one, Chris, drove an unnecessarily luxury car. I plainly knew they actually had lost a lot of money – these types of women are "huge *no no*" as partners.  I know not everyone will agree with me for the above three types I defined; personally, I had bad experiences with those three.  Although it is subtle, there are plenty of women trying to utilize a man.  Greedy men approach women more, so they fall into their own traps as a result.

Sexual desire is definitely a malediction for men, which does more harm than good throughout life.  In the best scenario, we can end up having a lot of kids thanks to it – which will bring lifetime drudgeries and money drains.  In the worst-case scenario, we can be one of those men committing suicide because of "Me Too movement," recently.  Or a man can be strangled to death in a prison like Epstein; some said he committed suicide, but it is possible he got murdered in prison, too; he knew too much secrets about other political figures.  I am not saying that they should live innocently, but that they shouldn't have dug their own graves *unnecessarily.*

\* \* \*

I don't think it's really worth getting married more than once in our lives.  My mother had been married once and she has me and my brother.  We can try marriage for experience once.  And, hopefully, most will have good marriages at first try.  Yet I think it is foolish to keep repeating it only because the first one did not work out.  Everyone has his or her own good and bad points in characteristics; there is no woman way better than others or having good points only.  According to my experience, it can take a decade to find a flaw in our partners. A single life can be better than a married one, so there is no reason to struggle to get into a relationship. If that happens, that's fine – it's nonsense to wrestle to get into a prison (marriage) to spend more money.

It's pointless to crowd our life with a wedding debt, bigger mortgage, auto loans or more kids to feed – no need for these, especially when the population is growing fast[8] nowadays. *We can all die together at this speed of growth* since the Earth has limited resources. If you are a man, remember this: **There is no terrific woman only having advantages.** There is no woman way better than our current or previous wives. If anyone thinks there is, the person must not have an understanding of human nature. Statistics solidly show that second marriages fail more than the first.

The least we can do is to check brides' character when we get married. For instance, I hate loud noises[9] and so does my wife. It is crazy if we don't check to see if there is a major discrepancy. I believe only greedy or stupid men approach women up to the point they get hurt. As a result, they never stay above minimum wealth level just

---

[8] The human population will be 9 billion by 2040.
[9] While I worked at the video game store, Jazzercise, an aerobic place for grandmas, moved into the next door in 2011; they made an incredible amount of noise. I have trauma from loud noises even now because of it. It was the stupidest business I have ever seen as new generations go for quiet exercise like yoga or meditation. Those three female owners made only noise pollution to hurt my ears instead of money; two of them were divorced women. The business was slow, lost money and moved out eventually after wasting a fortune. Dance club moved to that location in 2016.

like the dishwasher. Trump is still a poor old man among the super-riches after going through two divorces – we don't have to live in agony like that.

* * *

## Summary

1. It is pointless to keep chasing women.
2. One marriage for life is enough.
3. Smart men know there are no wonderful women existing.

# Being Unnecessarily Busy

*Working for money more than we need:*
*Financial gain, life loss.*
-Brad Kong

The poor are busier than the rich by nature; they often cannot buy a bulk of staples at once; buying things little by little takes more time and money. The impoverished parents tend to have more children, which makes them more engaged. They may have to spend more time with bankers to borrow debts for houses or cars; which costs *more* to pay interest in the long run and inevitably brings longer working hours. Some poor folks disguise themselves with luxury items. *When someone is oddly busy despite looking lavish, he or she may be under debt.*

Being slow can be a weapon itself when others are all busy. That is how sloths have survived or how turtles address fishes to catch. **Con-artists depend their successes on impulsive decisions made by victims**: *Hit and run*; they need to escape before everyone else figures out what's going on. If we process things step by step with enough time, less likely we will be a victim. When things don't go *right*, we can go *left*. Whenever things go wrong, I think the first thing we need to do is to stop and take some time to think. See if you can have 30 minutes to think alone everyday; not checking smartphones, but just closing eyes and meditating. Sometimes, "not doing anything" is the most prolific; I read our brains function to the maximum when we stop moving; people start thinking only when there is no movement.

* * *

I think rich people are *slower* for reasons. The virtue we need when we are poor may be diligence: *Hard working,* which means moving fast. But I think that "not being greedy" is more important after we reach beyond average: Self-control or abstinence, which allows spending less and having enough time not to do anything. **People often get confused that making and saving money are the same things**; these are different or opposite. Some may be good at earning, but waste a lot until nothing left (e.g., some former NFL superstars); some people don't make a lot, but keep money forever (e.g., some heirs of corporation founders in Korea); most do not know how to make or save; only a few are good at both making and saving (e.g., my father), which is the reason why we hardly see rich people.

In my opinion, there are only two reasons why some people get busy: Poverty and greed. **Greed is the thing making even the wealthy unnecessarily busy and painful.** I believe only a fraction of people are actually busy making more, but the majority of us are busy spending more. The greedy waste more since there are things they want more; as a matter of fact, it doesn't even matter what the thing is; as long as they can spend money on it, that should be more than enough. Imagine there is a greedy man eating an extraordinary amount of food; he will be busier than those who eat one meal a day (me). Eating more requires spending more time and money naturally; gluttons are busier than diminutive feasters.

Being avaricious can be one reason why people visit a place like Hotel Atlantis in Bahama. I think visiting there only makes people busier without having a gain. **The acquisitive are weaker at temptation**; they just want more by nature, so if someone suggests anything tempting, they fall for it easily. All they get from the Bahama trip is virtually stress: waiting at the crowded airport, suffering in the airplane, killing time on registration in front of the hotel concierge, etc. When we actually calculate, tourists spend a surprising amount of time merely on transportations. I am sure there would be a difference between North and Central America (Bahama), but I doubt it would be huge: More likely a waste considering the enormous vacation costs. Some vacationers wonder why they are exhausted after trips and where all their funds drained.

\* \* \*

While the greedy are fatter in general, they tend to have more kids, too; maybe some have intercourses more or plainly wanted more children as they want more of everything. I assume some try to have more partners for physical relationships, more marriages or divorces as well. And here is one thing for sure: **These will be busier than others, after all**; they will be short of time or money.  They may feel important since they get requests from everywhere, including their children, partners, divorce court, lawyers, etc.  While they get busier, their financial situation will sink slowly.  We see those unnecessarily busy people all the time, including in real life, on TV or in magazines.  They may be proud, but is being busy productive or profitable?  **Not necessarily.**

There was a Chinese writer named Amy.  I found her book *Tiger Mother* in the Korean section of our local library.  I am a father, but, to me, it was nothing but an unpleasant manuscript to show off how her children are great and why all the parents should extremely control their kids even in minor detail: **A total nonsense**.  First of all, I like to mention that I will never talk about my child or post my family photos in public that way.  My wife has always been strongly against public postings and I think she is right in this case, which is what a responsible parent should do: Protecting my child, including her identification and privacy, to begin with.  I see there are people who do not know what shame is any more.  Showing my child in detail to make book sales?  Negative.  **Unbelievable criminals do exist**; posting my family will not happen with me.

Apparently, this writer Amy is a lecturer, lawyer and mother of two daughters looking uglier than her.  To me, here is her *second* mistake: *Being busy for nothing*.  This is

43

a common misconception: Working more is good. Nothing can be *farther* from the truth. *In effect, I think working less is good.* Whether we work more or not, we will all die within the next 100 years. Do we get awarded by Heaven since we worked longer while we were alive? No. Do we get paid more by God since we worked longer during our lifetimes? No. Do we get paid less by God since we worked less after we die? Of course not. Probably, no one gets paid anything after life. **If nothing happens or all the results are the same, working more is actually a loss.**

I found out that her two kids eventually went to law schools, too. I am just curious, but does everyone in that family need to be law related people? Can anyone be a doctor, Silicon Valley Ceo or something? A lot of smartphone app developers are young millionaires these days. In my opinion, the mother blocked her kids from the future by micro-controlling them – **this not only suffocating, but also less profitable.** Lawyers used to make money – not any more. I felt this mother blocked better opportunities for her children. Her kids can settle in relatively less income jobs from now. I guess I don't like this Amy woman since she reminded me of my over-concerning mother in Korea. Mom has been wealthy, but also super controlling. Even now, I tend to keep some space from others desperately.

My wife has one daughter while this Amy woman has two. A lot of people believe that a two-kid family is ideal, but raising two children is way harder than one, according to my observation. I don't think any single person understands it, but I know since I have taken care of my daughter myself for years, especially when she was a baby.

**Do we get a medal of honor since we have two children instead of one?** No. Do people respect us more if we have two children instead of one? No. Do people admit or comfort us if we are having a harder time with two? Not necessarily. Will my parents be far happier if I bring them two grandchildren instead of one? Less likely. Do we get a lot of money from governments if we have two children instead of one? The simple answer is *no*. Unless we are extremely poor, we virtually get no advantage. We get a bit of tax deduction for one more child, but I do not think it is worth it since there are also people not paying any federal tax. In conclusion, I may end up being busy for nothing if I have one more child; I can work more for nothing. In fact, it can be worse than nothing since humans have destroyed the Earth gradually; producing less humans can be good for everyone.

\* \* \*

Some are getting poorer while getting busier for nothing. Getting fat is another word for having been busy eating for long – being busy pointlessly again. To tell the truth, it is also worse than being pointless. People can lose vision, limbs or kidneys as a result of diabetes. **Some get worse as a result of being busy.** When we are busy, at least, there should be a beneficial reason for it: A good reason, which must be better than nothing. Amy above reminded me of a woman I had conflict with when I had my business in 2012. I originally opened my game store right next to an internet cafe in 2006. Unfortunately, the cafe had to close out since no customers came in after high-speed internet started to be available at home. After the vacancy, to my surprise, Jazzercise aerobics for elderly ladies took the space. I believe that the young generation of girls don't do noisy fitness any more, who I notice usually go for quiet meditation, yoga or pilates. To me, it was a pure mistake to choose the space to start an exercise, to begin with.

**A smart business owner usually chooses a space where a similar business was occupied before.** For example, a lot of new restaurants open in old restaurant locations; they can use all the facilities the previous owner already built in, that way. It costs a lot to construct a new gas line for cooking, for instance. If there was an old restaurant before in a space, the gas pipe must be connected there already, so we do not have to spend money on that. Besides, we do not have to build a new spring cooler system, customer's restroom, etc. Previous owners can even leave or sell refrigerators or fryers for new owners; it takes some time to sell all equipment before the closing out date. Depending on the situation, previous owners just leave them and go. We can use all those and save money.

Then, I just didn't see anything in common between a computer cafe and aerobics. I remember they spent a lot on demolishing and reconstructing the whole aerobic business. I still wonder why they chose that spot, particularly. It was really out of the blue since the lease of the cafe was not over completely. I did not like these three old owners from the aerobics since they made *huge noises* from the day one they moved in. They did not spend any money on soundproofing for neighbors. I had conflicts with them for months and the plaza owner gave me a rental discount as a result. My store rent started at $1,200 a month in 2006 and went up to $1,500 a month by 2011. Then, it went down to $1,100 from 2012 as a result of the remedy.

I still recall a strange thing, though. After the property owner asked me to talk to Chris, the owner of the exercise business, she sent me an email saying that, "My schedule is empty between 10:00 AM to 11:00 AM. So I can talk with you during that hour." What is this? We all know that she is nobody and the business barely had enough customers. Why did she act as if she was super busy? **Being busy shows nothing but poor time management** in most cases. Or we will be busy if we are broke and desperate for a few bucks.

\* \* \*

Lately, I learned that Napoleon passed away when he was only 51. It seems he used up his life super efficiently; he conquered most of Europe and became emperor during his short life. **I think we can be busy only when there is a good reason for it.** When I checked Chris's Facebook later, I found out she was a divorced woman with three kids. It also showed she was remarried with a man having his own three kids, so it seems they have totally six children in their new household. This is another example of *being busy for nothing*: Being busy supporting double the amount of kids by failing the previous marriages somehow. Personally, I am already exhausted with one daughter and don't think I will ever do what her new husband did even with a *Miss America*: Marrying a woman with three children.

Rarely, some put themselves into busy situations since they are nervous about not working. For example, my wife cooks and cleans a lot. I definitely appreciate that, but I feel she is nervous since she has not had a real job for years now. She can take it easy for a while as we can afford her unemployment without a problem. I think I am busy writing since I do not attend a physical job any more, too. This writing brings some money, so I guess it is better than not doing anything. **Being busy itself won't make us VIP.** As Marx once said, "Free time is the space for development," after all.

\* \* \*

### Summary

1. Being busy can make us poorer.
2. When we are busy, there should be a good reason for it.
3. Being busy for nothing is merely a sign of poor time management.

# 23

# Eating Too Much

*Eating is a recurring charge.*
-Brad Kong

Ben Franklin once said, "A penny saved is a penny earned." Actually, this is wrong in my calculation – more likely, "A penny saved is two pennies earned." Why? After making some money, we always have to deduct tax and other expenses to make that amount: commute costs to work, car maintenance, new clothing, shoes, haircut, etc. We don't have to deduct anything from the money saved.

When we try to save money, I think the best strategy is to **address the biggest expenses first** (for example, housing). I heard that some rents of one-bedroom apts in CA are over $3,000 a month; I am paying an association fee of $367 a month in the Midwest in 2023 as I have owned a one-bedroom *condo*. The quality of life in a one-bedroom apartment and condo are similar; in fact, a condo is quieter, according to my experiences. I think I had been in 9 rental apartments in America for 14 years (1999-2013). CA apt residents pay almost 10 times more a month than condo owners, which is the reason why I keep suggesting buying out even a small home in full.

The second thing we need to address in saving is recurring charges: I think eating is something we *repeat* every day.  Eating too much causes all sorts of chronic diseases these days (e.g., diabetes).  Whenever I go to the supermarket, I am surprised at how much food people grab in their carts.  Many of us eat too much as if the food is free – in some cases, I understand EBT cards they use are free.  Still, eating is actually more expensive in America than other countries due to higher cost of living. I think reducing portions is inversely proportional to the chance of being wealthy; which means **the less we eat, the more we get affluent.**

\* \* \*

It has been seven times that I could not eat anything in Chinatown Chicago.  I occasionally go there as I live near Chicago.  What I mean is I couldn't choose one place out of 100 Chinese restaurants there and ended up eating some pizzas or salads right outside the town (usually at Ricobene's).  One of the main reasons is most menus they push to sell are meat-oriented; I am close to a vegetarian. I saw that some foods they advertise on the wall are boiled poultries in water, which smell yucky, according to my experience.  If not, 30% of eateries are some sort of desserts including bakeries there; these include too much sugars in common, so I never eat those for my tooth decay.

On top of that, I just don't see a self-serving place in Chinatown (like McDonald's); I don't want to pay an extra

20% tip only because someone brought food to the table. I saw a couple of places similar to our local takeouts not requiring tips, which were still more expensive; there is no point to eat the same food for a higher price than in my hometown. Furthermore, the town has always been dirty in general; truthfully, this has been the biggest reason; I lose my appetite before considering eating.

On the contrary, I notice that **I always eat something in India town Chicago whenever I go there**; I have been there probably 15 times so far. There is an Indian Pakistani concentration near Devon and Western and it has nearly 50 restaurants. First of all, I found that a lot of the menus in that town are pretty much vegetarian oriented. It's hard to make vegetable dishes disgusting; it is safe to eat, too; I am sure more food poisoning happens with meats or seafood everywhere.

Secondly, I like the chai tea from India; the ingredients are cinnamon, cloves and ginger; all of which are known to kill tooth bacteria. More importantly to me, the area has plenty of self-serving places. I pay, get food myself and save 20% tips. Some owners may think that customers don't have to pay up to 20% necessarily, but that's not what diners think. In the movie *Reservoir Dogs*, some gangsters talked about tips saying, "Throw a buck," which is not a buck or quarter any more. It would easily be $15 tips for meals of a few people and guests want to save on it: Some owners never get this point and go bankrupt. Lastly, almost always Indian restaurants provide plenty of free water in visible spaces.  Not only free, water is the most healthy.

From the point of *profit*, I am sure Indian restaurants make way more than Chinese counterparts.  **Food costs for vegetables are cheaper than those for meats or seafoods while menu prices for both restaurants are similar.**  Indeed, Indian foods are almost always more expensive than Chinese because of rarity I believe.  Neehee and Annapurna are new self-serving Indian vegetarian franchises and are getting popular now.  I saw the owner of Neehee once and he was happy to smile to the maximum.  I thought it's because of the crowds of customers, but there could have been another reason: Higher profit margins of vegetable dishes.

* * *

People just eat too much these days; these include Koreans.  I was shocked when I learned that it's common for Korean households to have more than one refrigerator nowadays.  The size of a Korean family is typically small.  **My wife said my mom in Korea also has three fridges at home;** she lives "*alone*" although my brother used to live with her for a while.  I lived with her until I became 26 by 1999 and we had only one fridge then; our family of four people lived in a luxury condo, so I do not know what happened.  FYI, my family of three (wife and daughter) has only one fridge in America now.

Overeating causes all sorts of diseases from toothache to heart attack, which only bring more hospital bills. The number of diseases caused by eating much are millions: *Obesity can even cause mental depression.* It shows that primate humans used to eat occasionally just like wild animals do now. Nowadays, some do that by controlling their portions and eating habits (e.g., intermittent fasting); they end up saving tons of money as well though that may not be their primary concern.

I personally have tried to eat only one meal a day since 2018; this means eating only dinner to me. I have lost about 30 pounds in the last three years; still, my target weight is 120 pounds[10] (55 Kg) while I was 125 when I measured it last time. I feel better for myself as I look better than before. **I have always felt bad after eating since I was born.** I will keep insisting on eating less as long as I can.

Our body is the most valuable asset and I believe taking care of it starts with eating less; it's great if we can make our bodies attractive rather than just keeping them healthy, which is achievable by eating less. Some studies show that people's income can be proportional to their attractions; in other words, a handsome guy makes more dough. **There is no way we cannot try it since eating less does not cost any money.**

\* \* \*

---

[10] 5' 6" or 172 cm.

There used to be a restaurant named "My Sweet Kake" near my home; it was a hand-made cake shop for weddings and birthdays and closed permanently in early 2019; I think it had been in business for about six years. I always thought that I would try the place at least once – not much, but at least one cupcake and a cup of coffee. I am not interested in those types of foods in general, but **I thought that I could help our local business once.** But I was lazy and the visit never happened somehow until on the day the business was closed out.

Subsequently, what I learned was that it was beneficial for me not to try the place at all. I ran into a huge tooth problem in 2019, which cost me a fortune[11] to have a crown on my molar. Naturally, bakers use large amounts of sugar to make cupcakes, which is detrimental for teeth; also, coffee is acidic and bad for oral health, too. It was great not to spend extra money on making my teeth worse; not much, but having one less cupcake and coffee must have helped my body a little bit. When I think about it, everything in our life is something like that: **Eating a little less during our lifetimes helps**; 70% of diseases are caused by eating too much.

* * *

Personally, I never go to an upscale restaurant; I may not have much money, but I just don't feel comfortable, nonetheless. Besides, I know there is nothing much we expect – virtually, we get the same foods on a fancy plate.

---

[11] $2,500.

I know this because I had worked in upscale kitchens for seven years; I think I observed how foods are prepared too well; people spend too much on meals and hospitals are getting crowded as a result. I have been admitted to hospitals twice and lost a lot of money in the last 15 years. When I think about it now, **the reasons for both admissions were eating too much.**

I was in the emergency room of St. Edward for a kidney stone in 2008, which cost me over $5,000 without having insurance, then. The reason was drinking too much soda (particularly, Coca cola). I was in dentistry for severe tooth pain, which cost me $3,000 for a crown procedure on a molar and extra in 2018. I had eaten sugary stuff without suspicion by then. I learned that **drinking a lot of water is important both for kidney and teeth health.** Nowadays, I strictly drink only water for beverages on any occasion. Although I have changed my eating habits greatly thanks to these incidents, I used to eat a lot and was fatter[12] as a consequence.

I think that there are few signs of being greedy: Eating much and being fat is one of them. We can hurt other lives on Earth by consuming them a lot; we can hurt ourselves as well as a result. There is a book *Food Governs Your Destiny* by Namboku Mizuno, the prominent Japanese astrologer and facereader. It has been a super-seller in Korea even though it was written 200 years ago; it does not seem to be popular in America even though I could find it on Amazon. The author tries to

---

[12] 165 pounds by 2010.

focus on being humble by eating less: **Small eating changes our destinies better;** he meant it is hard to achieve success in an uncontrolled covetous life; simultaneously, it is easy to lose everything in there, too. Always being modest is the key, which *starts with eating little*, according to the philosopher.

I have always wondered how my father made a fortune while both of his sons didn't make a lot. He had been drinking and smoking and caused a lot of trouble, especially by the 1990s; he got divorced as a result about twenty years ago. He is not supposed to be well-off, according to theories. **One thing I know is that he eats really small**, which has made him skinny for life. I wonder if this could have been the reason as described by Mizuno.

Another book that affected me greatly is *One meal a day*[13] by Yoshinori Nagumo. I know there are similar books, but I believe this guy is truly original – he is a licensed surgeon and research doctor in Japan who published it in 2012. His father was a doctor as well as it is a tradition that many sons inherit their fathers' professions. He said his father was obese and passed away from a heart attack; he got a similar symptom himself when he became middle-aged, which was the reason why he started researching food science.

---

[13] I saw that this book's title is *1 Day 1 Expression* on Amazon, which is the wrong translation.

The book concludes that humans have lived with hunger for over six million years, but we suddenly eat too much these days, which causes all sorts of medical problems. When we stop eating foods for a few days, he explained that our bodies start eating fat in our body, which we call "losing weight." But, **when our bodies eat our own cells,** more crucially, **they selectively consume tumor and cancer cells first.**

It is possible that we have cancer cells in our body all the time since humans have seven trillions of cells and mutations occur every day. Simply, if we do not give our body a chance to eat out some of the tumors, we are actually accumulating cancer cells in our body, which can bring horrible cancer someday. **No machine can detect and eliminate cancers at the super microscopic level as our bodies do.**

\* \* \*

I have lost a lot of weight, especially after 2018. I used to be up to 165 pounds by 2006, but I am 125 pounds now as of 2023. Then, I have read various books about fasting from the library; *The Complete Guide to Fasting* by Fung was particularly helpful. I learned that people don't die only because of skipping some meals. **Theatrically, we can live without food for 90 days, which is what Buddhist monks do during religious fasting period in Korea.** When I think about it, I don't really remember the last time I saw a news that anyone died purely by hunger. Statistics show that gunshot wounds and car accidents are two biggest causes for death among adolescents in America; certainly, there was no hunger on the list. I guess people usually can end up eating anything before the 90 days are over.

My weight loss started seriously with a root canal infection in 2018. Shamefully, my lower left molar had severe decay, so I had to spend close to $3,000[14] to get a crown on it at the dentist. I was stupid to eat anything, but my diet has changed drastically since then; I have cut off a large amount of processed foods, carbohydrates and all of the sugar. Most noticeably, **I cut off all the drinks except water** which is the only liquid I put in my mouth ever since. I occasionally chew gum (sugarless and aspartame-less) as I heard xylitol is good for teeth.

I started trying to eat one meal a day from 2018. I found that skipping breakfast and lunch has been much easier for me than dinner. I carry dental floss in my shirt pocket all the time, so I can floss whenever I feel like. I do oil pulling frequently – swishing olive oil in my mouth for 10 minutes. I usually spit oil on the grass in case I am outside, so it would not leave a mark. You would not believe how much money I invested in quality toothbrushes and pastes lately.

Unfortunately, the root canal infection problems remained on that tooth for about three years; I tried to cure it with natural holistic methods. The medicine I was

---

[14] It included a few other procedures, including deep cleaning for entire teeth.

taking was Padma Basic from EcoNugenics, which is a Swiss company and its herb drug had good reviews on Amazon. It helped, but couldn't cure my tooth infection completely. The tablet was invented originally for heart disease, but some said that it worked well on root canal infection.

$$* * *$$

I remember that the book *Holistic Dental Care* by Artemis was greatly helpful in 2018, which has perfect reviews on Amazon. **This book strongly suggests Japanese natto and miso soup as remedies for dental infection**: I tried and found out that these foods have been striking painkillers due to beneficial bacteria from fermentation. I understand Americans may not be familiar with Japanese foods in general. I have to confess that I never had tried natto before reading it myself, too.

The science behind it is that the slippery enzyme of Natto[15] helps blood get into the infected tooth. Our tooth is actually a living organ having long capillary vessels inside. While blood includes an immune system fighting infection, once the root part of the tooth swells due to infection, blood cannot get into the tooth smoothly. Blood entry to the tooth can be blocked and the tooth starts choking as a result. Natto is extremely lubricious and helps blood get in the infected tooth. **I witnessed that my swelling on the gum disappeared as soon as I ate natto.** I have never felt it is tasty, but I was able to

[15] NattoKinase.

eat all I bought.  Nattos definitely work on my teeth though expensive brands[16] taste better.

Luckily, Chicagoland has a few Japanese supermarkets having restaurants inside: Mitsuwa and Tensuke Market in Arlington Heights.  I saw some Korean supermarkets have them in stock, too.  These are usually under $4 for three packs in 2023.  When I tried it with Miso soup, it was even better.  Instant miso soups are $12 for 30 packs and we can have it right away with boiled water within 2 minutes.

I did not like the Indian lady dentist since she suggested pulling the tooth out right after my crown procedure in 2018; she mentioned it right after I spent $3,000.  She could not find any crack on the tooth with x-ray initially, so we proceeded for the crown.  I believe there are more frauds in dentistry than other medical fields – too much competition and student loans makes them desperate.  It was my mistake to have my molar rot without visiting a dentist for long.  I am eliminating my sugar consumption more than ever now – I guess it will be like this until I die.

* * *

## Summary

1.  Eating a lot gradually makes us poor.

---

[16] There are hundreds of Japanese brands.

2.  We should not act as if groceries are free; these are actually more expensive in America than other countries.
3.  Intermittent fasting has been helpful for my finances and health.

# 24

# Not Living Long Enough

*We need to be alive to gather our harvests.*
-Brad Kong

It sounds weird, but I think some people died broke simply because they did not live long enough. Occasionally, it takes longer than expected to get rewards out of our hard work. **If we die too early, we just miss the chances to get paid.** When we die too early, people in the future may describe that we had a poor life and died broke – the truth is that some must have passed away before pay days. Critics concluded Van Gogh was an unfortunate artist. He had lived poor, but a lot of his masterpieces have been sold at high prices after his death. Nonetheless, not many realize that **he passed away at the age of only 37.** What could have happened if he lived until 60? Probably, he could have enjoyed some money for the last 23 years of his life. What if he died at 100? It's possible he would have died as a millionaire.

On the contrary, Pablo Picasso has been considered a billionaire artist: **Did you know that he died at the age of 91?** More importantly, was he rich at 37? Wiki shows that Picasso was also impoverished in his earlier life, which is common for painters. We need to live longer to get famous, which is the general rule of thumb.

I can take Lucia Berlin as an example for writers, who never really got known during her lifetime. She had been married three times and had been a grappling single mother with four sons. She was a smoker for life and died in poverty at 68 in 2004. However, suddenly she got an award and became prominent in 2015 after Straus & Giroux published a collection of her short stories titled *Manual for cleaning women.* **She would have been 79 if she was still alive by 2015.** She died of lung disease due to smoking, but if she lived until 100, she could have enjoyed larger royalties for the last 21 years of her life.

Warren Buffett is 93 years old now in 2023. Was he extremely rich at the age of 37? Not really. **I think it is important to survive through the brokeness until we get to the next level.** *Psychology of money* by Housel explains that more than 97% of Buffett's wealth has been accumulated after his age of 65.

\* \* \*

A lot of humans are able to live until 100 with medical advances these days. With the rising trend, I think it's important to start four things ASAP to get affluent: education, travel, house purchase and getting interests. Suppose there is a boy learning how to speak English at

10; he can use the language in the next 90 years. Imagine I try to master Spanish by next year; I can use the skill only in the next 49 years at the maximum. **Clearly, starting early has an advantage in education:** We can use the same knowledge longer. The same goes for travels; people can learn knowledge out of the experience. The earlier we go somewhere, the longer we can use info from it.

This is true for home purchase as well. If we do not have enough money for a small condo, that is fine; we just need to save more. But I think buying a big house with a mortgage when we can afford smaller ones in full is *nonsense*. When we free ourselves from a rent or mortgage early, we can start accumulating wealth early, too – it is proven that time is the most valuable asset in building opulence. Having debt for long will only bring us more debts in the form of compounded charges, so getting out of it quickly is the key. Also, the same goes for getting interests as incomes; during our lifetime, getting dividends for 70 years is better than for 30 years.

\* \* \*

I think people perceive thin women as attractive instinctively – which is the reason why supermodels and idols are skinny. And, this is a *great* thing: Why? This makes humans eat less overall. Therefore, I think a little less animals, including livestock and fishes, are killed, as a result. Have you seen photos of old people celebrating their 100th birthday? No one is fat among them: being skinny is being healthy, after all. **Being able to live longer and keeping money for long matters wealthwise.**

I had thought about this question seriously a few years ago: If I have only six months left, what should I do? Definitely, I will not work a second more. Maybe that is why I resigned from the nursing home job finally in 2022; things had been getting worse there every year compared with in 2015 when I was hired. There was no reason for me to endure unfairness, especially from the short disrespectful Mexican sous chef, while I have more than enough money. I didn't want to play the nice guy forever: A wealthy guy who still wants to help elderly people despite unjustness? That's not exactly who I am and having a rude coworker was such a pain. Some think they will live 40 years more when they are in their 20s: Is 40 years a long time while 6 months is short? When we think about it, 40 years may not be that long: Human life is short, basically. **In a sense, we all have only six months left in our lives.**

* * *

I recall that the Mongolian husband of my wife's girlfriend died at 38 from liver failure in 2007; he was a heavy alcohol drinker. I heard he was the youngest son for his parents and his two *older* brothers visited his funeral: Certainly, **there is no predetermined order for who passes away first** though there was an order for who was born first. If he is alive, he would have been about 54 years old in 2023. His wife has three kids and the man was an auto mechanic; I heard that he had worked double for decades: a regular mechanic for his day job and his own auto repairing business in the evening (he renovated his garage for it). Some drink crazily after working long hours: Still, **he would have not worked double if he knew that he would be gone at 38.**

Some people start dying of lung cancer in their 50s. I believe there are more smokers in Korea and a majority of them start the habit as soon as they get into college; it could be three decades of smoking by 50, which is my age in 2023 and some would have already died. The same goes for drinking as alcohol is a prominent carcinogen causing cancers. If anyone dies at the hospital bed by 50, one of the most predominant reasons is any type of cancer, according to my observance. Otherwise, it can be any disease related to obesity (i.e., stroke or heart attack).

Since a lot of people die while we don't notice, I think being alive after 50 is a success in a sense. I think we should be proud if we are old and alive now. I am not exaggerating; I mean it. If anyone has never lost any tooth by 50, it is more than a great success in my opinion; I have lost one so far and plan not to lose any more until I die; it has been my new goal and is really possible since many achieved this. I have been drinking only water strictly for years as it is the sole liquid safe for teeth. On top of it, I notice it's good for my kidneys and weight loss as well.

\* \* \*

I don't think we should be frustrated only because of finances, especially when we are young; don't commit suicide for it. According to my experience, money never comes evenly throughout our life. **People usually spend, waste or lose more in their earlier lives.** Being short is common when we are young even when our parents are rich, while we usually make and save more later on. There are three mandatory reasons for this. First of all, education costs a fortune and it is mostly concentrated early in our lives. It usually starts with kindergartens or elementary schools and can go all the way up to postdoc in our 30s. **We cannot make a lot of money while we are in school.**

Secondly, people usually get curious about the world and travel more at early ages: **Travels cost a whole lot of money.** As they get old, they usually settle in a place and do not move around as much; old people are not fairly curious as they checked out everywhere already. No adventure means no unexpected spending, so people tend to save more later on. Thirdly, all of us will go through a trial and error period somehow. We should not blame ourselves because of the mistakes we made so far; this is just a part of our lives. Yet, unfortunately, **errors can cost money and happen more during the early stages of our lives.**

I lost more than $2,000 for nothing only during the time I was in Cornell University in 1999. I had to move out from a shared apartment before the 1-year contract was over since I had three horrible roommates. Except meeting my wife, who eventually earned a doctorate degree with scholarship in UIUC, nothing good happened in the city of Ithaca; I am not sure if it was the school, the city or me.

First of all, the English language school (IEP, then) at Cornell was bad: Super expensive, but poorly managed compared with others. It had poor classes, faculties and activities in 1999. When I was in R.I.T. in 1997, the school even helped all the students get social security cards. One officer came to a classroom and issued one for every single student. I did not realize how important it was at that time; when I think about it, it has been fundamentally important up until now. I appreciate Mrs. Cone, who is retired, and would like to thank that she did a fabulous job overall.

Secondly, Ithaca was a small town with a 50,000 population then and did not have enough housing for students: Low quality ones at super high prices. When I studied at Cornell, I stayed in the dormitory during the summer semester in 1999 (3 months). That was when I met my wife even though she had to leave for a Master's degree in Arkansas after summer. I had to move out of the dorm after summer, but the language school did not give us any help. I had to find one crappy apartment shared with three others on my own. The three roommates were horrid: Ron from Grenada; Steve, an unpleasant Korean American from LA; a Japanese guy whose name I don't remember. I recall Ron was *especially* dreadful; facebook shows he is divorced and I clearly understand why.

Lastly, I didn't like the gloomy atmosphere in central NY very much. Ithaca was a small and suffocating city – plainly stressful for no apparent reason. It did not have a study promoting environment. I skipped school so many times, which never happened before throughout my life. I escaped the city whenever possible during weekends, vacations or holidays. I did not necessarily enjoy trips: I just wanted to get out of the city – these all cost my parents more, ultimately.

Particularly, I felt the shared apt was a hell and noticed that a lot of students moved out before finishing contracts. I found a one-bedroom apartment outside the city and moved out. Then, I got a strange letter from the management to pay all the remainder of the 1-year contract: $350 a month for the last 6 months[17]. I don't even know how they found my new address since tracking like that was illegal; my info was not even on the Internet since I stayed barely a year in total in Ithaca. I felt they are familiar with runaways. Since there was a rumor that a bad record like this can remain on credit, I decided to pay up and get rid of the worry for good. I felt sorry for my parents who had to sacrifice while they didn't even realize in 1999.

---

[17] About $2,000.

* * *

In general, I don't think I had much luck with NY State. Moreover, I found out that Illinois is cheaper and cleaner after I had visited my wife studying in Champaign dozens of times. The cost of living in Buffalo was similar to Chicago, whereas Chicago is bigger and more prosperous than Buffalo. As a result, I don't think anyone moves into NY State any more.

Nevertheless, I still thank SUNY[18] at Buffalo since it charged the cheapest tuition in the nation (cheaper than UIUC undergraduate); which was about $6,000 a semester without scholarship by 2005. The campus did not have fancy landscapes, but had plenty of places to study alone, including plenty of libraries and computer labs. All the exams were competitive, but I loved the fifth floor of the Law library as no one was there all the time. Additionally, I had a chance to work at the banquet in the school and its pay was helpful (thank you, Michael Kusinski, fat friendly Polish Banquet manager!).

I lost a lot of money until I became 35: rent, moving, business mistakes, etc, as you name it. Actually, money loss barely stopped only after I bought my condo in full at 40. **I am still frugal only because I obviously know I have wasted a lot in the past.** At least, I have never drunk or smoked, so money has been lost on experiences, not on health damage. All those include

---

[18] State University of NY.

unique Ivy League memories, after all. We just need to live long enough to get our investment back.

* * *

## Summary

1. We need to live long enough to get paid.
2. Some die too early before getting fortunes.
3. Living shorter increases the chance of dying broke.

# 25

# Not Having Strong Opinions

*We need to trust our instincts –*
*don't be fooled by experts.*
-Brad Kong

The more we get wealthier, the more temptations we will get: I think *"not moving by temptation"* is key to protecting our wealths. One way is that we need to be mature enough to know that there is **no point to feeding all our desires**; a lot of them are vain, pointless and disadvantageous. Have you heard of the *Broccoli test*? A lady wrote that it is one way to know if we are truly hungry or not – if we can eat broccoli, we are truthfully hungry; otherwise, it's just brain hunger. This gave me an idea; there is something I like to call – the *"Mona Lisa test"*. There is a well-known painting *Mona Lisa* in the Louver Museum and a crazy amount of people are always waiting to see it: *I personally don't find it particularly attractive.* If you feel like seeing it as well or urge to wait for hours only because others do, you may not have your own mind.

We are all subject to *crowd psychology* somehow and probably have done whatever others usually do without thinking.  For example, some of us might have bought crypto currency only because it *seems* popular.  But, there are others feeling that, "I don't know why bitcoin is so popular"; more likely these are the ones having sane minds.  I think it is critically important, especially when we do stock trading: **Frauds always use this crowd psychology to some extent.**  Simultaneously, I think recording our own opinions is important.  In a sense, the only thing we leave after we die can be our own articles. *The Diary of a Young Girl* by Anne Frank is one of the most printed books throughout history; she died only when she was 15 in March, 1945; she had the typhus epidemic in a Nazi Jewish camp.  **She could have been long forgotten like her sister who never left any writing.**

Christopher Columbus was the discoverer who found the "new continent," which is central America, in 1492. Yet he believed it was India until he died.  The record says Amerigo Vespucci was merely a small merchant from Florence, Italy then; nonetheless, he published a four-page book in 1503, which is 11 years after Columbus' discovery: "This is not India, but must be a new continent!"  **Now both the North and South American continents have been named after Amerigo**[19].  This was the power of writing; it's almost impossible to make a small street named after me, but he made huge continents named after him.

\* \* \*

---

[19] America.

Sometimes, I feel like I am a hotel manager; my ideas are like guests. I cannot squeeze ideas out of my brain, but I can accept those whenever they visit me. I can take care of my guests by writing them on the note. Whenever I am lazy, they go away and disappear often for good. The Roman emperor, Marcus Aurelius once said, "You have power over your mind, not outside events." Being sane is crucial – **being always awake in Buddhism.**

"Control is power," Schindler put in the movie *Schindler's List*. Whoever has stronger control over his or her mind wins; whoever has control over money cannot be badly off. In a sense, **having power is all about control**, which applies to building wealths, too. There used to be a Korean social site I used to go to. Virtually, I was the only one writing articles worth reading there as it had nasty trolls; they all had debts and supported their lavish lifestyle against common sense opinions. Oddly, in common, they never wrote anything helpful; at least, not something worth noting.

How can I avenge them for their offensive replies? The best way is not to write anything there any more – forever. It is Friday, so if I don't write anything until this Monday morning, I think that would be a tiny revenge; I know they will check the site millions of times to see if I write anything over the weekend; they will waste the whole three days until Monday – **making them waste their time is a torture.** They would feel stupid in this Monday since I am going to write about only the contents of my book series and release date, so they can buy them hopefully someday.

How can I plan revenge on trolls without breaking any law? I am the one who has control; I have control over whether I will write or not; they have never written any real articles; there is nothing they can do except wait for my writing. As long as I can control my urge to write, I can keep control over those losers. Certainly, I am not that strong to control myself reliably if I stay at home or near a computer to write. So I think I will walk around since the weather will be nice over this weekend. I will just bring my notebook and pen just in case any good idea comes to me.

* * *

An example of control over money is *not checking* the stock accounts often. When I think about it now, I should have put all the $90,000 in the Pfizer stocks in January, 2021. As I explained, I ended up getting $90,000 cash after selling all the Pitney Bowes shares; I made about +$20,000 profit then. Pfizer stock (PFE) was about $35 at that time; now it is $50 as of May, 2022, so I could have made more profit along with a 3% dividend. *I should have put all my money in there.* **It was a big mistake that I did not trust my own instinct,** which made me lose money in a sense. I was looking for a company bringing me a solid dividend after reinvesting the $90,000. Pfizer originally released COVID vaccines in 2020 and my wife and I got three shots respectively by

2021.  I thought that it's a great company making great products that will save the entire human race.  There were only two companies successfully able to produce COVID vaccines during the era:  Pfizer and Moderna.

I wasn't confident with Moderna stock since this *new* company never made anything other than a vaccine then. That is fine, but it was not preferable as an investment since it did not have anything to back up their loss in case that happens.  Both companies had to produce the vaccine ASAP due to the emergency; no one in my family had adverse symptoms, though.  **Moderna stock does not come with a dividend,** so I thought Pfizer stock is a better investment, which has been fine so far.  Only problem was that I did not have the strong courage to stick to my own opinion.

I have a stock account with Fidelity and its analysis kept saying that I had concentration in only Pfizer stock and it's no good.  Even before getting the $90,000, 6% of my portfolio was Pfe; I still had 98 company stocks and 42 company bonds by 2022.  Fidelity said they do not recommend putting more than 5% of my cash only in one company.  **When I had a hard time with PBI, it occupied up to 25% of my portfolio**; my portfolio was down for long only because PBI was down.  I thought I would listen to Fidelity this time and put only $30,000 out of $90,000 in Pfe in 2021.  However, it was a mistake when I think about it now in 2023 – I should have put it all in pfe.

Since I still had the extra $60,000 left, I decided to put it in bonds of diverse companies: Alphabet (Google), Apple, Amazon, Microsoft, Berkshire Hathaway, etc, which are the biggest companies in the world. **Many do not come with dividends, but their bonds always come with interests.** More importantly, I thought that economic depression would come sooner or later in 2021 as it was the third year after Covid broke out. **When a depression comes, stock prices generally go down while bond prices go up.** So I set up a new strategy: "Let me not buy stocks any more except Pfizer. Stock prices will go down one way or another. Let me buy bonds instead, so the total portfolio will not crash." It was supposed to be a fine tactic, but the problem was the timing. Luckily, stock prices did go down a lot, so I had to sell a lot of stocks when they were still high. The problem was the *massive amount of bonds* I bought after selling those stocks.

* * *

FYI, the bond prices are always $1000 for 1,000 shares (face value[20]) originally. Bonds are not like stocks: **Bonds keep $1,000 value in 1,000 shares all the time and we get $1,000 back when 1,000 shares of bonds mature in the end.** The maturation dates of bonds are all different. But, since we are guaranteed to get our $1,000 back eventually, it is extremely important to buy them cheaper than $1,000 initially. The bond commission to buy and sell is only $1 per 1,000 shares,

---

[20] The price that the issuer pays at the time of maturity.

which is called mark-up fee.  So there is no worry about losing a lot on commissions.  **Also there is no penalty to sell bonds earlier than maturation date**, which is the main difference between bonds and CDs.  In the case of CDs, if we break it before maturation date, we will definitely get an early withdrawal penalty, which is usually 6 months' interest.  Also we can easily buy them where we buy stocks like Fidelity, Charles Schwab, etc.

There is no guarantee for minimum back in stocks. **For bonds, we always get our $1,000 back as long as we wait until the maturation date.**  It is up to us if we sell bonds when the price is more than $1,000; in that case, we can make a profit and lose only $1 out of a commission.  Fortunately, I managed to buy all my 42 company bonds for less than $1,000 face value in 2021; for example, I bought the Google bond for $800 instead of $1,000 par value – this was supposed to be a *smart move.*

Nonetheless, unfortunately, the bond prices went down way more since 2021.  Why?  Suddenly, the Federal Reserve started increasing interest rates consecutively due to high inflation.  **High interest rates means people tend to put their money in the bank rather than stocks or bonds.**  The bond market especially collapsed more than stocks; Google bonds went as low as $510, which is ridiculous since it is supposed to be $1,000.  As a result, 65% of my portfolio has been in bonds and it is still down as of 2023.  I have never not lost money since I will not sell any bonds any time soon; I will

78

keep getting interest until they mature. But, **if I put all the $90,000 in Pfizer as my instinct indicated** in January, 2021, **I would have been seeing way more profit as it has been up, not down like bonds.**

\* \* \*

## Summary

1. Trust your own instinct.
2. Do not change your plan only because an expert says something.
3. Be aware of crowd psychology and stay awake.

# 26

# Living Recklessly

*We are the ones who make our own destinies.*
-Brad Kong

There are people living recklessly beyond necessity. I am not talking about taking risks for investments. Some just live flat-out dangerously; for example, some do skydiving as a hobby; some choose dangerous jobs like cleaning windows of skyscrapers, while having other choices. **Surprisingly, some just stand on a line between life and death habitually.** And reckless lifestyles cost money, including more hospital bills, and some stay poorer despite working.

Lately, I checked Wiki for other writers like Tolstoy, Dostoevsky, Marx, Dickens, Hugo, Melville, etc. When I tried to change my job to a writer in 2022, the first thing I was glad about was that I do not have a lot of kids to feed. Taking care of one child has already been hard for me, so my wife has done most of the work, including making extra money, which makes me a loser. I just do not know how other writers handle this issue in the beginning, especially when they have big families. These are the number of children they had: Tolstoy (13), Dostoevsky (4), Marx (7), Dickens (10), Hugo (5) and Melville (4).

To me, it is ironic that most of these writers had a lot of kids while they wrote about poor people. Hugo wrote *Les Miserable* and it is all about indigence. Dickens wrote *Hard times*. In the case of Marx, it shows that three of his children died when young and he wrote the *Das Kapital* criticizing the emerging selfishness from capitalism in England. The title of the first novel by Dostoevsky was *Poor people*. Melville did not write anything particular about penury, but had to borrow large sums of money from relatives after *Moby-Dick* was commercially failed. I guess **things could have been a little easier for them if they didn't produce a lot of kids from the start;** it must have been hard for their children as well. I assume they must have squeezed incomes when they were not known. And I learned that Dostoevsky lived a little more dangerous than others.

\* \* \*

Fyodor Dostoevsky (1821-1881) was born in a poor family in Russia in the 19th century and died when he was 59. He was the second child out of seven. And, unfortunately, both of his parents passed away by the time he was 18. I am curious, but isn't it common sense for a man to live a little more cautiously when he becomes an orphan without a parent? Oddly, he seemed to do exactly the opposite – living recklessly throughout life, especially after funerals. I am not talking about drinking, smoking or gambling, which he had done continuously. He had a whole new level of issue – **sentenced to death for going against the Tsar when he was 27.**

Dostoevsky was involved in anti-government activity against Nicholas I and spent eight months in jail before being scheduled to be shot to death in December, 1849. **The penalty did not proceed luckily since he was forgiven at the last moment,** which was mocking execution. He wrote about this experience in his book *Idiots* later on. Still, he had to spend the next four years in Siberian prison and an extra five years in army service, instead of a longer imprisonment (totally nine years for that anti-tsar charge). More unfairly, all these happened after he finished three years of mandatory army service as a lieutenant officer during his early 20s.

So when I calculated it, it seems he spent more than twelve years out of his fifty-nine years of life in army service or prison. According to my experience, the Korean army was like a mild form of prison. I think his 12-years was a long confinement considering being against the Tsar is not exactly an offensive crime (it may be a political crime, which is not a crime at all depending on eras). On top of these, Dostoevsky had four kids with a few women though two of them died early. He had been a heavy gambler, drinker and smoker throughout life. So now I am a little confused as to the reason why he lived in agony: Was he just unlucky or did he carry bad habits to be broke mandatorily? Obviously, he was a prolific writer, so if he lived with a bit of wariness, I think he could have lived a little easier and probably longer.

* * *

I wonder if the opposite example of Dostoevsky can be Tolstoy (1828-1910), who was another Russian writer born in the early 19th century. First of all, Tolstoy (82) lived far longer than Dostoevsky (59) despite their alcoholism in common. I know Tolstoy had thirteen kids with one wife, but I do not see any prison sentence, gambling or divorce record on Wiki. He might have met a wife like an angel. Or he just managed his life less risky, so he did not get into a divorce necessarily. As soon as I saw the portrait of Tolstoy, honestly I felt much more *peace* from him than Dostoevsky. **Apparently, Tolstoy had spent a quiet life in the countryside** without much conflict or trouble.

I believe we make our life *ourselves* and decide our own destinies – **this tendency gets stronger as we get older.** When we are ten years old, our parents' situation can decide our lives. But, when we are 40, whether we binge drink tonight or not can decide our wages two weeks later (I used to get paid every two weeks). It is a misconception that someone else *decides* our fates; there must be influences, but decisions will be made by us, which is going to happen even to adult children of rich people.

My father has been wealthy for life, but I started receiving a good amount of money from him only after I bought my condo in full in 2013. He was impressed with how I got this unit at such a low price. Maybe he felt confident that I won't lose his money at least. We have to win our trust and accumulate credits even for our own parents' expectations. I admit that it is lucky to have an oofy parent to begin with, but I don't think inheritance happens automatically unless we are an only child. I had to work for it – we may have to prove ourselves one way or another.

\* \* \*

The stupid Brazilian soccer team "lost" to the Croatian in Qatar World Cup in 2022; it's shocking that the Brazilian couldn't pass the quarter finals[21], which has been rare. This

---

[21] The strongest 8 team play.

is a shame for Brazilians since its FIFA ranking was #1 in the world by 2022; their team won the championship five times so far. It's even more astonishing that **the population of Brazil is over 214 million while that of Croatia is less than 4 million.**

This is what they did during the game with the Korean.

Here is what most people do not know. In my opinion, Brazilians lost since they overly enjoyed their success too early while offending Koreans. They had a game with the Korean (first round[22]) right before the match with the Croatian. They beat the Koreans 4-to-1 in the end, but whenever they had a goal, they danced offensively; that included their old, but thoughtless head coach, too. A lot of people, including Brazilians especially after their loss, found their acts disrespectful. Some people live like this for life and they never end up becoming successful: **Some cannot survive little successes.**

\* \* \*

---

[22] The strongest 16 teams.

**Being calm and doing things *step by step* can save us tons of money;** we should never get emotional in any case. The crown filling of my left lower molar came out a couple of months ago (October, 2022). Now I have to do fasting in the next couple of months (I cannot eat well for minor pain) and start looking for a dentist who can fill it up without upselling root canal or implants. Fasting itself is one way to cure tooth infection as well: When we fast, our bodies start eating bad cells inside our bodies; as a result, we lose weight. Some doctors claimed that a 30-days fasting can cure any disease. I would like to try that before spending another fortune on my dental treatment.

**I think *waiting* and *delaying* are good *strategies* on many occasions**: I think we can have everything or make our lives close to perfect when we use these properly. There are things we would better not do, but we want. See if you can wait until the urge goes away – it always goes away, after all. There was a house in Roselle I badly wanted in 2012; I am glad I did not buy it, especially with a mortgage. It could have been a terrible choice when I think about it now; my current condo is 1,000 times better and was 4 times cheaper.

There was a girl from an Italian immigrant family when I worked at the nursing home; she seemed to be popular among boys as many Italians are skinny and good looking. But I am glad I blocked my interest in her; she was a smoker, marijuana smoker and drinker; she had low education (high school graduate); she was rude and her parents were financial disasters to lose home due to foreclosure during the mortgage meltdown in 2010. My feeling persisted for a while, but finally it went away; now I can call the police if she addresses me. Don't do anything stupid with women; stay away from them if you believe they won't help your future; being in love can be nothing but a dopamine addiction in a physiology. Whoever we marry, we will get fed up with her and find someone more interesting; block the person unless she is a logically good choice. **One way to let the urge go is by delaying.** When you want something, see if you can wait and get it tomorrow; delay it a week if you can. Always remember – none of our desires last forever.

* * *

Have you ever been in a situation where a bunch of problems broke out together all at once? In this case, I think that it is important to keep tranquil and not to be overwhelmed. **See if you can solve the easiest problem first**; it may not be much, but still one less thing to worry about after solving it. Then, see what's going to happen next. Human minds are strange; sometimes, a good idea finally comes only after solving a problem; we just don't see it until the situation changes. The same thing goes for a math problem; sometimes, we have no clue to address a problem in the beginning. Every so often, a clue finally comes only after solving it to an extent. In real life, **it's better to see what's left after solving the easiest matter** since some issues can go away on their own as well.

I had 98 company stocks and 42 company bonds in my portfolio by December, 2022. Currently, I am losing money on two electric car company stocks: Lordstown (ticker: ride) and Workhorse (wkhs); I bought 100 shares of these at $4.00 and $6.50 each; it seems I may have to wait for a while to sell these out with profit; in other words, I have to wait until Lordstown stock goes above $4.00.

Workhorse does not update anything, but Lordstown updates their YouTube channel for its *Endurance* truck regularly. Logically, I believe "ride" will rise first. If so, I think it's better not to worry about "wkhs" for now. I do not know what's going to happen, but let me focus only on selling off Lordstown with profit first – *it's pointless to worry about two problems altogether.* Technically, I have more than enough money; I just want to get rid of two stocks bringing me a headache. **I think it's better to focus on solving the easiest issue and see what's going to happen next.** *Realize* that many of us actually have more than enough money and have overly accomplished things – no one needs to rush for anything.

* * *

There is a novel *The Alchemist* by Brazilian author Coelho. This is an excerpt: "You will spend the rest of your days knowing that you didn't pursue your Personal Legend, and that now it's too late." This is an instruction the alchemist gave to the shepherd boy. Santiago tried to give up finding his treasure and the alchemist urged him not to by basically saying, **"If we miss the opportunity now,**

**we will never be able to find the treasure again.**" I understand there is timing for everything, but there are things I do not agree with in this book. Quite frankly, the reason why I bought this book was because the author made a lot of money[23]; it was flat-out boring till almost the end; it was merely a story of a shepherd boy trying to go to the Pyramid for treasures, but finding out that those were buried in his hometown.

It seems this is what the author is trying to say: "Do something if you really want to do it. You won't be able to do it forever if you keep delaying." This is occasionally the wrong lesson, according to my experience. I used to be like Coelho in my 20s: Doing as many things as possible during my lifetime is good; accomplishing more goals, making more money, getting more degrees or whatever. Now I think a little differently: "We have to leave everything when we die: **Everything we use is borrowed.** We do not necessarily have to do many things. If we can do it, that is fine; if we cannot, that is fine, too. I think it is perfectly fine if we live our daily lives just as we do now. Unless we commit a crime, we have the right to live peacefully. We do not have to look for more gains or treasures all the time."

Nowadays, a lot of people, especially advertisements, ask us to do more things; we have to go to Cancun for vacation, we need a Harley Davidson to ride, we are obliged to get a new girlfriend like Swift, so we can check her music videos every day. **None of these is necessary.** A great Korean monk said it is perfectly fine if we focus only on making

---

[23] It shows that his net worth is $500 M.

ends meet until we die; don't worry about those people saying we need more.  Worrying about our salaries or living costs in housing are enough – we will indeed get happier when we do not diversify our attention to many things.

* * *

## Summary

1.  Being boisterous can make us fail.
2.  Some live financially needy since they live dangerously.
3.  Being daring is not always good.

# 27

# Preventable Medical Problems

*Smart people solve problems.  Geniuses prevent them.*
-Brad Kong

I personally think those corporations making candies are criminals against humanity; these include the companies selling chocolates, liquid candies (sodas), fruit cans, cakes, cotton candies, etc.  **Did you know that alcohol and sugar share very similar chemical structures?**

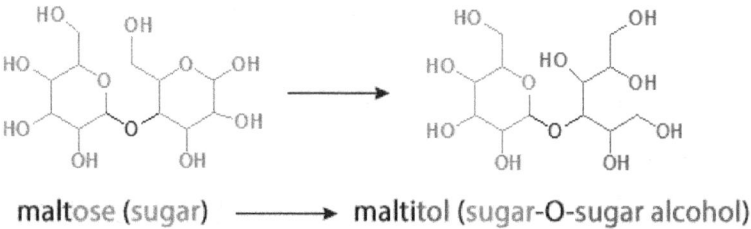

maltose (sugar)  ⟶  maltitol (sugar-O-sugar alcohol)

Yet alcohol is restricted in most societies; besides, many people know that it has no good taste, instinctively.  Personally, I have been a nondrinker for life purely because I do not like the flavor.  But, in the case of *sugar*, most folks, especially children, do not know how *detrimental* it is to our teeth and bodies – they just eat sweet stuff since it tastes good.  **Mass productions of**

**sugary stuff are the worst thing we can do for our children.**

I had a root canal infection on my molar when I was 45 in 2018; I had an unimaginable pain suddenly while I was eating my fruit for lunch one day; most people describe it as the biggest pain they have been through.  My friend Frank said, "It hurt like hell."  If anyone saw me on that day, he or she might think I was crazy:  **I just didn't know what to do to get out of the acute pain from the molar in my jaw.**  I went to the bathroom and kept squishing my mouth with warm water for 20 minutes and it went away finally.

Mercifully, I have spent most of my life without knowing how painful a toothache can be.  I thought a tooth is like a sort of stone without having a nerve in it and it is ok to eat chocolate bars as long as I brush my teeth everyday.  This is why sweets are sold everywhere and people eat them all the time, right?  My father brought expensive ones whenever he's back from foreign countries.  If manufacturers knew all about those pains and damages on bodies and still make them for money, they are simply immoral: A shame.  **Not eating sugar can save us tons of money out of medical bills.**  FYI, I used to own Coca cola stock, but sold all the shares after the incident.

\* \* \*

I think one of the most common wastes on dental issues could be the implants: these will be useful for missing teeth in visible locations. But many dentists just recommend implants no matter what only because these are *profitable*. Finally, I lost the molar tooth which I had crowned on by extraction in September, 2022; I had struggled to save it for four years. Amid agony, this is the only tooth I have lost by 50; it was just too late to revive, to begin with. I was stupid to mistreat all my teeth for over three decades. Regardless, when I checked Quora to see if a molar dental implant is necessary, this is what I found: **No medical reason at all to have the missing premolar replaced by implants.** It seems implants are pretty much for cosmetics.

I have lost two large sums of money on medical bills so far: Kidney stone (2008) and root canal infection (2019). I worked in my own business then in 2008. After being in the emergency room for the stone, I removed all the soda from the store cooler and filled it up only with bottles of water. I would say that I have drunk only water for my choice of liquid since 2008. I didn't know at that time, but it must have been helpful for my teeth as well – only water washes out sugars from teeth. Nonetheless, I had a tooth infection in 2019, even after drinking only water for 11 years. I should have cut out sugar and carbohydrates aggressively since only drinking water was not enough for decay prevention. I have brushed my teeth reasonably in the last 50 years, but it has not been sufficient. **I believe limiting my diet is the only way, which can save me tons of money from now.**

In real life, the surest way we can save from medical bills is taking care of teeth. I recall I have spent at least $2,600 on the molar from 2018 till 2022: X-ray twice ($200[24]), Inlay crown ($2,200, 2018) and finally extraction ($200, 2022). However, if I decide to have an implant on the empty gum space, it will be another $3,000 at least (totally $5,600 only on a molar tooth!): **The issue is that I still have 27 other teeth left in my jaw.**

Drinking only water for life and getting rid of sugary stuff completely are priceless strategies – I admit we may not be able to eat 70% of the food we used to eat this way. Still, what's the point of eating unhealthy foods only to get fat? Eating only food good for teeth can save us not only from medical bills, but also from incredible pains. How can a dentist charge a huge bill? It's because patients are willing to pay: Why? Root canal infections hurt excruciatingly. I think being interested in health issues and reading related books can save us $ millions literally. I found out that **many diseases are chronic and preventable these days.**

\* \* \*

I think there are three things we need to do on a daily basis to be healthy: eating small, sleeping a lot and taking extra care of teeth. When we focus on keeping our teeth clean, we get healthier throughout our bodies in general. There are three things we must do to keep our teeth clean everyday: **brushing, flossing and oil pulling.** We

_____

24 Special X-rays outside for consulting.

need to consider losing a tooth is like losing an arm. I recommend doing intermittent fasting for our teeth on a weekly basis as well (no eating one day a week). On top of it, not eating anything 12 hours a day (basically overnight) truly helps our health overall; this should be easy since 8 out of those 12 hours would be sleeping.

Food wise, I think the Thai are the worst for teeth to me. I know Middle Eastern desserts like Baklava cram sugar inside, but I just do not eat those. Thai put sugar directly into major dishes like Pad Thai, which is unusual for other countries. Processed foods in Mexican supermarkets (e.g., Cermack) are terrible for teeth, too; I notice they put more sugar even in drinkable yogurt (some people choose kefir to cure teeth, but it won't work with Mexican brands like Lala). Have you been to a Mexican supermarket yourself? In common, I notice that these have more sugary stuff than others; grocery shopping in Latin markets must be avoided if that's possible. Korean and Chinese foods are not really beneficial as well, while I assume Indians are relatively safer for teeth. I learned Chai tea has a lot of ingredients to kill tooth bacteria: cinnamon, ginger, clover, etc. Although Japanese foods are not generally good for teeth, I learned **their nattō and miso soups are excellent for dental cure.**

Mental wise, I think there are three ways to live a happy life: Being satisfied with what we have, accepting who we are, and having easily achievable goals. For example, **can I just be happy with the fact that I am alive now?** It doesn't matter how much money I have; I am tired of pushing myself to achieve $1 million in my portfolio. Why do I need more money, anyway? To fulfill my ego? So I can confirm that I am better than others? If I forget about feeling superior today, maybe I can be happy today. There are plenty of people who pass away before they become 50; some become disabled or lose more than a tooth, too.

As far as goals go, I like to have something other than the financial one: I think I can try to live until 100 and preferably, I like to walk on my own until I die; I like to keep all my natural teeth. Finally, I have reached more than $650,000 in my portfolio as of 2023. Oddly, it hadn't made me delighted for more than a few months. I still look for 50% discounted sushi at the supermarket after 7:00 PM. Will I be much happier if I have $1 M? **Probably for a year.** I like to be satisfied with different types of accomplishments I made so far; for example, I have a wife and child. Having a family is an achievement as I see some have never been married or even dated. I have seen some Korean lady trolls lately, and I don't think these single women will ever have a chance to meet a decent guy (they are too old, to begin with).

* * *

The crown in my molar, before losing the tooth, came out when I chewed gum in Sept, 2022; I immediately thought that the Indian lady dentist deceived me in 2019. I paid close to $3,000 in cash since she said it was a crown; it was supposed to be less than $1,000 since it was actually an inlay. Regardless of the costs, she just did not

96

do her job well.  Another old mold I got from Korea came out before, but it was after having it for over 25 years; these are supposed to stay for life.  This inlay I got from her only stayed less than 3 years.  **I believe more overcharges happen in dentistry rather than other medical fields.**  I read countless books and web articles regarding dentistry afterwards.  To be fair, the Indian lady's deep cleaning service ($800) was helpful.

Nevertheless, this is what I concluded:  There is *no real cure* in dental offices; all they can do is basically the cleaning and cosmetic changes.  **I conjectured that the only way to prevent decay is not eating sugars and carbohydrates, to begin with**, which is certainly the basic.  My diet has changed greatly since then, including drinking strictly water.  I check sugar contents first before buying any food and often don't buy it if it has sugar.  Also I started eating omelets, kefirs, cheese and natto, which protect teeth.  Coincidently, this habit has helped weight loss and diabetes as well.

\* \* \*

It shows that medical bills are the #1 reason why people go broke in America.  **The most undervalued factor for health is sleep** in my opinion.  People do not realize how crucial it is only because we sleep every day – the same as we do not perceive how important air is.  To me, there can be a few things that disturb good night sleep.  Certainly, we may need a quiet place with a firm mattress, first of all.  For example, smartphones or physical pain can disturb sleep. **Beyond all, I think it matters not to have anything to worry about**; for instance, some people wake up in the middle of night for debts, including a mortgage. Moreover, I think we should not go greedy for anything if it can bring any anguish unnecessarily.

I suggest people sleep enough, instead of doing anything else – **it doesn't cost money, anyway.** It is nonsense to spend time on hobbies while we don't get sufficient naps. Scientists suggest lack of sleep can induce dementia, as well as Alzheimer's, later in life – it includes a complete memory loss including our names. Margaret Thatcher was the former Prime Minister of the UK. She was a well-known short sleeper; it shows she slept about four hours a day. She suffered from dementia and stroke for about 10 years before she passed away at 87 in 2013.

Johnny Yune was a successful Korean American comedian; his net worth was about $15 M by the time he passed away at 83 in 2020. I watched his show a few times on a Korean channel (Johnny Carson show in Korean version), and he once joked that he couldn't not get enough sleep since he had to work to death in the beginning of immigration; people often asked him "Johnny?", which means "sleeping?" in Korean. I thought it was just a joke since old Koreans tend to exaggerate their hardships – *it was not*! He was actually diagnosed with dementia in 2017 and the news says he could not even recollect his own name before died; this must be a severe case among the patients, though. **I think**

**sleeping now is important since consequences can come decades later.** Additionally, taking care of vision saves a lot of money; I have wasted tons of money on glasses and contacts in the past thirty years. Lately, I invest a good amount of time taking care of teeth every day.

* * *

Men may like pretty women, but I don't think they necessarily prefer a woman having cosmetic surgery; they are fond of naturally beautiful girls and most females know it already. When they get plastic surgeries, I heard that some Korean women look for surgeons who can perform the procedure without leaving a mark – **these chicks want to look natural and will pretend they never got it;** they lie that they never had a surgery when someone asks. This is more than deceptive: *Pathetic* in my opinion.

Having plastic surgery itself is dangerous for women; every surgery is precarious. Some ladies not only spend money on risky surgeries, but also they have to hide the fact that they had them. I mean, how low can a human go? Why do they have to sacrifice that much? Were they ugly? Or do they care for others' eyes too much? Or they have never gotten any attention before? None of these seem to give me a positive feeling. If possible, just stay away from these types of women. I honestly do not like super insecure women. The top category of women I will never date would be the ones having plastic surgeries; they are often in vain, too. If a man marries one of them, he can be more likely a human ATM for her lavish consumption until he gets a divorce.

While plastic surgeries on the face are popular among Koreans, it seems those on the body are more popular among Americans and Mexicans. It shows that breast augmentation is the most common procedure in America. **If a woman gets breasts by an implant, what is the difference between a man and woman?** I heard the silicones for augmentations are toxic to bodies; reports show that some women fainted for no reason and found out that they had fungus on silicones in their breasts.

The most ridiculous surgery I have witnessed was that of a Mexican young lady who got buttocks augmentation. I actually saw this on TV twenty years ago and still cannot forget about it. The doctor asked her to be careful whenever she sits since the silicones can *burst*. I truly wonder why she got it since every woman will get fat butts for one way or another; at least, my grandma had ones. Besides, it is such a turn off for me – I have ever been attracted to a fat girl, to begin with. After surgery, I saw that she ran to a bar with friends. I wondered why life seems to be so easy for some though her family did not look wealthy. **More than half of plastic surgeries seem to be failures from my perspective:** I hardly see a woman who looks beautiful after those. Not rarely, some look worse than before; I am not talking about long term side effects. I believe many procedures are just wrongfully done from the start.

\* \* \*

Some people say that hospital bills are too expensive in America: They are wrong! – these are expensive everywhere in the world.  I do not believe there is any country providing quality healthcare at low price; most likely it is not quality if it is provided for free or at low.  A good example is free healthcare in Canada; I heard old people die even in the hospital aisle while they are waiting for a doctor; some get only a couple of Tylenols after eight hours waiting.  It seems it is the same as not having a hospital: **If it is free, it is seldom a quality one.**

I was in the emergency room at a hospital in Naperville, IL in 2008; I did not know it was a kidney stone.  The pain was searing, so I thought it was something more serious.  I stayed there only for five hours, had a couple of CT scans to confirm the stone and got Vicodin[25] and water – these all cost me $5,500 total, then.  It was an unnecessary big spending, especially when I struggled with my rent.  **I had to pay up to three different rents for six months, then**: my store rent, apartment rent and my wife's apartment rent.  Soon, she and I found a small one-bedroom apt near my store and moved in together, so three rents became two[26] in 2009.  Still, I had to pay these two for eight years and three months (from 2006 to 2014).

---

[25] A pain reliever.
[26] An apartment and a store rent.

No wonder I have trauma about paying rent. Including the store rent for 8 years (2006-2014), I had paid all sorts of rent from 1992 till 2014. Initially, I moved out of my parents' home to go to college in Korea in 1992. Yet I have never moved back for diverse reasons: college, army service, immigration, universities, my business, employment, having my own family, etc. I finally bought my condo, so rent has *gone for good* since 2013. So, basically, I had paid rent for 16 years in my 20s and 30s except for the army service. And this was my calculation: "Suppose I live until 100. I had lived in my parents' for the first 20 years of my life rent free. Then, I paid rent for the next 20 years (except the military service). After that, I bought a condo when I was 40 in 2013. If I live here for the next 60 years, **I end up paying rent only for 16 years out of 100.**"

Personally, I am glad I did not go up to the point of getting a mortgage. Technically, there is nothing wrong with home loans, but there was a Korean troll who did not know what shame was (he's always on the website). He never wrote any constructive articles, but always posted nasty comments on others – **coincidentally, he has a *huge* mortgage.** My hatred about the mortgage has started and grown mainly because of him I assume. Maybe this is good since a mortgage is not necessarily beneficial for personal finance. Conclusively, I had changed all my diet, including quitting soda, which caused kidney stones, permanently, after the emergency room visit; I did not expect to lose so much weight only by cutting out sweet drinks. I removed all the drinks in our store cooler and filled it with only water that year.

* * *

## Summary

1. Medical bills are the #1 reason for personal bankruptcy in America.
2. A lot of diseases are avoidable these days.
3. Drink only water and eat small.

# 28

# Unnecessary Legal Problems

*Some lawyers just want to make money.*
-Brad Kong

O. J. Simpson is an American former football player, actor, and broadcaster; he was a top star, especially during the 1970s. It shows that his maximum net worth was over $10 million[27] in the 1990s, but it is estimated at just $3 million as of 2023. Most of us probably have heard of his trial in 1994, but that was not all. Unfortunately, he was also involved in tax fraud and armed robbery in Vegas, subsequently. I cannot mention all, but it seems he has had diverse types of legal troubles against law enforcement every few years. And here is one way I found we can avoid them.

One day, I realized that we do not have to take revenge on anyone. Sometimes, we see people we really don't like. Rarely, we cannot forget some of them and think about getting revenge on them. I learned we don't have to do that. **If someone was aggressive to us, most likely the person lives a miserable life by now:** Why? He or she must have been annoying to others, too. When I

---

[27] About $20 million value in 2023.

was in Cornell in 1999, I didn't like one of my roommates in a shared apartment. All three were not that great, but one black guy Ron from the Caribbean was the worst; I remember he was way more rude than the average African American I have seen in America. Lately, I checked his Facebook and learned he was divorced. I did not like him and apparently his wife didn't, either. Probably he's paying alimony pointlessly now. I didn't have to take revenge on him: he screwed himself – he will keep doing that until he dies.

When I was working in the nursing home, I particularly didn't like a woman cook. She said she is half Mexican and Cuban, but very rude to all the dishwashers, including me; she was a single mom with three kids then. She kept making trouble and eventually got fired from the work by 2019. When I checked her Facebook lately, I saw that she was taking care of two extra babies looking similar to her. To me, she ruined her life – now she has five kids from three different men and none of them is staying with her. **This woman screwed her life completely.** As a father myself, honestly, I can say no man is excited to support five kids as it's highly stressful. No need to get revenge on anyone: I am sure she will never stop ruining herself until she dies.

There were Korean trolls going against my frugal lifestyle on a website. The best revenge is letting them live as they have – the debts, including credit cards, mortgages and car loans, will ruin their lives. I will keep living humbly and keeping my overhead small, so I don't have to get back to being offended in the working places again. **I think one of the biggest wastes in our lives is lawyer fees due to a legal dispute.** I remember I paid a $3,500 lawyer fee[28] around 2001 – it was definitely an unnecessary loss, especially when I was broke then.

* * *

I don't think the smart get into legal trouble; they know it costs money, so many tend not to commit anything against the law from the start. The stupid not only get into trouble, but get caught easily, too. An example was George Floyd, honestly. I know some try to describe him as a scapegoat from police violence or even *worship* him as a hero: Nonsense in my opinion. Did you know that he had been arrested 11 times, convicted of 8 crimes and spent more than 5 years in prison? He died right after using a fake bill, which is another federal crime. Some wrote the officers planted a fake bill to cover their crime in Quora. Why would deputies choose an extremely tall (6′ 4″) black guy only to bully on? I am not saying that he deserved to be dead, but he was not purely innocent as protesters claimed, either. He ain't Jesus Christ and it is absurd to praise him beyond reason. **There are plenty of African Americans working hard despite unfairness.** My black friend E[29] has been an industrious cook for life, but always struggling economically. Bitterly, things didn't work out for him for reasons.

---

[28] This would be like $7,000 in 2023.
[29] His real name is Erskine, but everyone calls him E.

Another example is Giacomo Casanova (1725 – 1798), who was a Venetian adventurer and author in Italy in the 18th century. Probably, most of us know him as a playboy. Yet did you know that he was sentenced to 5 years in prison and spent 15 months in a dungeon for a sexual crime? He kept having similar problems throughout his life and had to move from one country to another to escape charges until he died at the age of 73. He must have been a genius to get a doctor's degree at University of Padua at 17. He had made a fortune a few times, but spent it all on women, including prostitutions. Additionally, he had been in jail a few times more due to being unable to pay debts[30]. Finally, he got Syphilis in his mid-40s and had been sexually inactive for long. Being alone, he died penniless in Duchcov, Czech. Getting involved in a legal problem may not help anyone, including the plaintiff; still it would be worse for the offender.

Bikram Choudhury is the founder of *Bikram* Yoga, which was reaching a peak of 1,650 studios in more than 40 countries by 2006; Choudhury's net worth was estimated to be up to $75 million because his highest salary was $10 M a year by 2006. Unfortunately, it shows Choudhury has not been in America due to a rape charge since 2017; it is almost like he has lost his $75 M assets since his business foundation has been in America. By 2014, five women had sued him with allegations including sexual harassment and assault; he lost $7 M for fine in the courts and decided to return to India forever to avoid more charges. In 2016, Choudhury's attorney stated that

---

[30] Going to prison for debts was common then.

he won't return to the U.S. to defend himself from other pending court cases. **It's a ridiculous way to lose an entire life savings this way**; he should have controlled himself a little before being kicked out. An interview shows he used to live in Beverly Hills, CA; I hope he enjoys warm weather in Calcutta, India by now; that's where he's from, but incidentally, it is known to be the poorest part of India near Bangladesh.

* * *

The stupid commit more crimes; the smart know there is no way we can escape from it nicely these days. **Often, committing some crime does not benefit anyone, to begin with.** Taking drugs is a crime, but regardless, it does not benefit us health wise. Above all, drugs are not free – nonsense to spend money at a cannabis dispensary even if it's legal. I recall it was 2001 when I had a legal problem for the first time in my life. I hope it will be the last time since nothing has happened in the last twenty-two years. I was still a student at UB then.

**When I think about it now, the most effective way to decrease the crime rate is lowering the unemployment rate.** I had a job at the banquet on the college campus that time. For some reason, they never gave me enough hours for months. In fact, they never gave me any hours at all during the whole winter vacation. I was still in my 20s and eager to make money to support myself. I tried to study over the winter. Still, I had too much time to kill while my bank account was getting empty. If I was busy with some jobs or lived with my family, nothing would have happened.

Now jobs are available everywhere due to the pandemic since 2022 – "Help wanted" in every restaurant. I am pretty sure the crime rate will go down as well; people do not have time to think about committing a crime when they are busy making money. It sounds ridiculous, but we actually need free time to do wrong things. Besides, when we have enough money coming in (i.e., wages, salaries, tips, etc), there is less reason to try something wrong to make more money. I think that *crime usually happens when people have too much time, but no money* in their pockets. **Nothing is more important than providing more jobs and lowering the unemployment rate for social safety.**

\* \* \*

Anyway, I ended up spending $3,500[31] for a lawyer fee and $125 for a court charge in 2001, which was a huge loss to me. Ridiculously the court did not give me any fine – they disregarded the entire case only with a court fee payment, but the lawyer fee was huge – a total waste of money. I know the lawyer we hired didn't do much in my case. Some assume lawyers are good people and try to help innocent people accused wrongfully – nothing can be further from the truth. In real life, probably those who got charged may not necessarily be innocent, from the start. Then, a lot of private lawyers try to take advantage of

---

[31] This amount could be about $6,000 value in 2023 after inflation.

clients' situations as opportunities to make money. I am sure some lawyers are benevolent, but I did not have a good experience with a couple of them. I would say the lawyer Mark did not do anything and took my $3,500. It was my fault to cause trouble, to begin with, but I will learn it has been the most ridiculous way to waste money. *Getting a lawyer itself is a financial punishment* in a sense. Maybe that is how the legal system works – **criminals get punished financially by hiring lawyers, regardless of court results**.

There are reasons why hard workers get broke despite working full-time. I could find many examples of some staying in the low income class because they keep causing legal matters. I heard OJ Simpson lost almost $10 million only for lawyer fees in the 1990s – some lose their life savings for legal defenses. It's unlucky if a legal situation happens for inevitable reasons we cannot control. But, in real life, disputes or crimes happen because of greed. I believe a lot of conflicts can be resolved before going up to a court if we are less avaricious. **Crucially, not having a legal problem is not just for money.** I had to visit the small town court three times in 2001 and felt nervous and stressed out all the way over the course of six months. Worrying about a case had broken my nerves and been a mental drain as well.

\* \* \*

Today I got a letter from the State unemployment office saying I have to pay them $1,200 back since my *unemployment case* cannot be qualified as a "laid off." This is not a legal case, but I read people can go to jail if they cannot pay the office back, which is the reason why *I sent them a check* immediately. Initially, I applied for unemployment benefits only because the HR from the nursing home sent me the information package right after I resigned from my job. I didn't even expect I could get unemployment benefits. Anyway, I applied as they suggested and the State approved it, so I got $1,200 in the last month. I applied for a "laid off" case since a new company Morrison came and took over our department. I was blocked from being transferred to it (which I am glad about, later). But suddenly this IDES sent me a letter that I am not qualified and needed to recoup the money; I sent them a $1,200 check right away. **If I delay, the amount will only get bigger.**

Still when I think about the benefits, I feel Illinois State is stingy. I have paid Illinois State tax without skipping in the last 17 years. They obviously know that I had worked at the nursing home for seven years and the stated job was dishwasher, typically giving a meager wage. They cannot let a retired dishwasher keep $1,200 when the person is resigned by the condition he couldn't control? Should I really have to pay it back? I paid $1,500 State tax only for the last year – **I think they are miserly**.

In my opinion, one legal way to fight against high tax and government parsimony is living in a smaller house. The property tax in Illinois is the second highest next to NJ in America. I know a lot of big houses pay over

$10,000 property tax a year in my town. Yet, oddly, **when it goes to townhouses or condos, property taxes drop significantly.** I paid $1,700 for my one-bedroom condo last year, which was like saving $8,000 out of taxes legally; it can be $400,000 savings in the next fifty years.

I do not have a car now, but I think I had been in traffic courts about five times when I had them for eighteen years (1999-2017): three times for high speed, one time for a stop sign violation, etc. The total fines accumulated were probably over $500. Besides, I had to pay for parking tickets at least 5 times if not more – the total might have been over $300. **All those had been a waste**; I wish I had the $800 in my pocket. Some get DUI violations or accidents, so fines can be higher as it shows DUI violation penalties *start* up to $2,500 in Illinois. Avoiding a legal issue is definitely a way to stop draining money.

* * *

## Summary

1. Getting along with others and avoiding troubles saves a lot of money.
2. Committing a crime is a reason to be broke.
3. Drug related crimes are stupider than others in finance. Some thieves at least make money, but those addicts don't make any profit out of consumption.

# 29

# Talking Too Much

*Speaking one less word may save our lives.*
-Brad Kong

History records that the Sun King in France, Louis XIV (1638 - 1715), was a quiet person – a man of few words. He was the most powerful emperor throughout French history ruling for 72 years, who had the Palace of Versailles built for himself. It shows he usually listened to his officials completely, and often said only a word, "I shall see[32]." Then, he ordinarily walked away; the ministers and courtiers would never hear a word from him after that, but only see a result by his action afterward. Greene suggests that not letting people know our intention by speaking less gives us more power in his book *The 48 Rules of Power*. He described that **Louis' silence kept those around him terrified and under his thumb.**

When tsar Nicholas I ascended the throne of Russia in 1825, rebellion broke out immediately and they demanded modernization of Russia in the 19th century. The leader of the rebellion is a poet Ryleyev; unluckily, he was caught by the Russian army and sentenced to death in 1826. On the

---

[32] In modern English, it is translated into "Let me think about it."

day of execution, Ryleyev was hanged, but blessedly, the rope around his neck broke, so he saved[33] his life that day. Then, this is what he complained: "The tsar doesn't even know how to make a rope properly." At that time, it was a common practice to pardon a prisoner who saved his life somehow when execution went wrong; kings believed it's a sign from heaven. Before signing the pardon paper, the tsar asked a question.

Nicholas I: Did Ryleyev say anything after this miracle?
Messenger: He grumbled, "Russia doesn't even know how to make a rope properly."
Nicholas I: In that case, let me prove the country.

Ryleyev was hanged again and *died* the next day. This is just an example, but I had countless moments myself saying something awkward and regretting it later. When I think about it, miraculously, there is no moment to regret for not saying a thing. **Whenever I wonder whether I should say a thing or not, I conclude that it's *always* better not to say.**

\* \* \*

I found out that speaking and eating less are common traits among monarchs staying in their positions for long; in a broad view, these two are virtually the same things. There was a king Yeongjo in the Joseon dynasty in Korea in the 18th century; he was known for eating small and had

---

[33] Actually, it said that three out of five prisoners saved their lives due to broken ropes that day.

reigned the peninsula for 52 years[34]. He died at 82 in 1776, which was considered a long life then as Louis XIV died at 76 in the similar era. In a sense, living longer means hurting more animals as we eat more of them that way. I am curious if we tend to live longer when we hurt less animals, which includes becoming a vegetarian. It shows that Queen Elizabeth II in the UK has been in position for 70 years since she passed away at 96 in 2022; she had been known for her frugal lifestyle. **It seems things like speaking, eating or spending too much are all from greed.** I determine we should not be greedy to live for long.

Making noise is like smelling a bad odor; some people, especially women, do not realize how bad it is. There was a girl talking continuously in the library the other day – thoughtless. I tried to go to the library early in the morning since there are less people, but a chubby computer assistant kept talking – not loud, but continuous. I truly wondered how some can move their mouths nonstop for hours like that, which is impossible for me. And I am glad my wife and daughter don't do that – they talk when there is a need, which is fairly normal I thought. **I didn't know it's such a blessing until I met other ladies.** I have never heard a man say, "I love a talkative girl"; the opposite is true in real life.

I quit the weekend nursing home job in 2022 since I did not like a *sous chef* there. He talked too much and interrupted others whenever he liked – no one liked him.

---

[34] The longest in Korea.

He said his family had been on food stamps before he got the job (being a sous chef job is no big deal, but still a manager in a kitchen).  Stupidly, the first thing he did after getting it was leasing a Lexus with a loan.  I got a gut feeling that he may be destitute for life despite working day and night.  I think fasting from talking could be more important than eating: **A mute never creates an enemy.**  When things do not go well, I think we should live without talking for a while.

* * *

I recognized that there was a common characteristic among those who have worked for dishwashing over 30 years: They talk *unnecessarily* a lot.  I had always felt they talk far more than cooks or chefs, who get paid more.  Pancho and Enrique used a cell phone to talk more; just killing time on excessive talking seemed to be their daily routine.  **I eventually reached a conclusion that moving mouths without a point is a lifelong habit for losers.**  I saw a poor old Mexican sitting in the middle of the library the other day; he talked on the phone bothering everyone; some never look for a book to get better even while in the middle of a library – only talking surrounded by plenty of new books.  In a perspective, I think his life is already over; he will probably continue his painful, repetitive, low income job until he dies.

All the religions, including Buddhism, Christianity and Hinduism, have a fasting and silence period on each own.  I am not a religious person, but I always try to welcome those habits; I am skinny, but I am trying to lose weight more. If we are serious about getting out of hardships, I think the first thing we need to do is talk only when it's necessary. When we talk, often we stop thinking or moving. Words are tools, not toys, especially when we are at work. Only a few know how to control their mouths; many of us make noise with voices. **Moving mouths without thinking not only makes us poor, but can put us in danger.** Knowing how to close our mouths could be the most important life skill.

There used to be a time when being careful with our mouths was enough. That happened probably before the invention of a letter, which is about 3,700 years ago. However, it is the digital age now; we ought to be careful with our fingers as well. **Not only speaking, we have to be cautious with our writing and photos.** Luckily, I have never posted my face photo in public, including this book. My wife and daughter do not have social media accounts, thankfully. I used to write a lot of articles online and something happened in 2009.

* * *

There is a popular community site called "Dcinside[35]" in Korea; it's similar to "Reddit" except that everyone should post a photo to publish an article; the popularity of the site was so big that it had 200 million clicks a day. It is considered an underground site with hundreds of sub-categories divided by topics; they call them

---

[35] Digital Camera Inside.

"sub-galleries" since it started out as a digital photo site. I used to go to the *small business gallery* since I owned a business then in 2009 – *Cyb Knight* video game store (2006-2014). I wrote an avalanche of articles regarding how to improve businesses. When I think about it now, I have been interested in "how to upgrade finances" for long. Nonetheless, I was stupid since I had written precious columns for free interminably. If I knew anything about self-publishing then, I would have published myriads of books by now.

The problem was low quality trolls gathering on the site. High unemployment was a national pain in Korea by 2009. In particular, a lot of young people could not get hired and the media mocked that the new generation gave up finding a job, getting married and buying a house – "Giving up the big three" generation. Frankly, I have always thought that South Korea is a hellish place to live by nature; its territory is as small as Indiana State – virtually, an island surrounded by the sea and North Korea. 70% of its region are high mountains, so the space people can live on is even limited; 52 million South Koreans are trapped in a tiny space. As a result, **we can't see a single family house in Korea any more.** Virtually, everyone lives in a type of sky scraping condos or multi-units, regardless of their wealths. It has been overly crowded physically.

On top of that, the country does not have many natural resources like oil. To make things worse, the political situation has not been friendly, either. It is encircled by aggressive neighbors, including China, Japan, Russia and

North Korea. I was raised on the 13th floor of a tall condo when I was a teenager and never liked it. I learned I have acrophobia later on.

*  *  *

I started to write about my business and what we can do to improve it from 2008 – about two years after I established it in 2006. Then I realized some readers were those who used to own businesses and failed them. Small business failure rate is notoriously higher in Korea than America for several reasons. First of all, real estate costs, including store rent, are much higher for business owners in Korea: **Rents are expensive mainly because too many people are crammed in a tiny space.** The most popular locations are on the first floor of a building and they could not build more properties forever in a limited area.

Secondly, I believe that the lack of diversity causes higher business failures in Korea. America has more diversity in ethnicities, languages, religions, foods, etc. While we do not notice, **American businesses are more unique since its residents are from all around the world.** For example, Korea does not have Taco made by Mexican or Falafel made by Turkish, whereas America *has* Kimchi made by Koreans (95% of the population in Korea is Korean). Diversities allow business owners to avoid direct competition from the identical businesses, which makes them more *compatible* to survive. Suppose that there are Mexican twins building exactly the same Burrito restaurants, respectively. One built it in a Mexican neighborhood having dozens of taco stands; the other built it in a Japanese neighborhood having no Latin restaurant at all. Whose business can survive? The situation of the first boy happens in Korea nation-wide.

Thirdly, the lack of creativity among Koreans is the reason. Actually, the Korean education systems have been blamed and criticized for oppressing the creativity of students for decades; they said current systems make students only good at memorizing things. While there are not as many high school dropouts in Korea as in America, it has not been necessarily good news for the country, ironically. In consequence, we see factory-manufactured dull adults there; proportionately, **we see too many cloned businesses in Korea.** I am not talking about franchises, which the country has plenty of; Korean businesses are more independent, yet many copied each other to be exactly the same.

I think that I am the only Korean who has owned a GameStop type of business in America ever; most Koreans own restaurants, laundromats, hair salons or groceries here. I am the only one who married a foreign woman among my high school colleagues since they all marry only Koreans. This trend causes another reason why Koreans are not good at small businesses.

Fourthly, Korea has a weird culture that people can be blamed for if they are different from others: **Koreans are *afraid* to be different.** Millions of them all start Ramen houses together when the menu is on trend. They all start coffee shops together when it gets popular. Then, they all go bankrupt and close out businesses together as well. I saw some Koreans complain that, "It is how it goes in the world as everyone is in the same situation"; which is simply not true. I guess some feel comfort from the fact that everyone does the same things like a sardine in a shoal of fishes. Sometimes, it shocked me that no one even tries a little variation in his or her own business.

* * *

Anyway, those failed business owners started to leave nasty comments on my articles on Dcinside anonymously; I assume they were jealous. I should have quit writing by that time in early 2009. But I was elated that a lot of people read my writings; 10,000 clicks on my articles were common. I think I was born with a strong desire to leave a mark as many carnivores do it. Only issue was that I did not forgive nasty trolls all the time; I *counter attacked* them occasionally with replies. Then, they did a mean thing.

Those losers found the address of my business and started ordering food to it – prank calls for delivery to the store location. I had to let a lot of delivery guys go back without paying them (I was broke). The great internet cafe customer guys helped me by taking those foods a few times, though. They were generous to say that they were hungry, paid for some deliveries and ate the food. I truly appreciate Lance and Steve, the second owners of the DMZ internet cafe next door; they always said, "We can take those foods, instead of ordering somewhere else." That was decent of them; I truly wish my best luck and remember them as the best people I have ever met.

At that time, my wife called restaurants around to warn them about the prank calls. But, in the end, a Korean troll called 911 and falsely reported that there was an oven fire in my store. A fire truck came in and left briefly after checking there was no fire. Subsequently, the police said they will try to find out who the caller was with the IT team. I never wrote on that site after that even though my articles could have helped countless entrepreneurs. I am not sure if the caller was caught eventually. All I found out was that this kind of prank calls are increasing internationally and fines are not small. Above all, **I will never understand people wasting time on something not bringing them profit.**

I started writing books, instead of online now. If I write four pages a day, it would be six hundred pages only after five months out of a year. I guess I can write a 600-page book a year. I will write about the poverty solution for a while, but eventually I may end up writing a sort of diary. Most don't recognize that diary is a surprisingly popular genre: *Diary of Anne Frank, Diaries of wimpy kids, Dork diaries*, etc. Nevertheless, every article I write will have points and a conclusion.

\* \* \*

## Summary

1. If we are not sure, it's better not to say a thing.
2. People generate noise pollution while they do not realize it.
3. It's a serious disease to talk continuously without having a point.

# 30

# Spending Too Much on Pets

*I hope we can help all the lives on Earth.*
-Brad Kong

This chapter is dedicated to my old cat, Oscar Yang (2003-2020):
*Born on the street, buried in the wild.* The day I adopted him in
Buffalo, NY in 2003; he was 3 months old; the paper box was from
Erie SPCA.

The day we buried him in a Chicago suburb in August, 2020; he was covered by my sweater, which was his favorite; he died of blood cancer at the age of 17, which was 86 in human age.

Jocelyn Wildenstein is a Swiss socialite known for her *feline look* due to extensive cosmetic surgeries. She divorced from the billionaire art dealer Alec Wildenstein, which brought her $2.5 billion settlement in 1999; it shows that she spent over $100 million a year for the following 13 years to fulfill her lavish lifestyle and eventually filed Chapter 11 bankruptcy in 2018. There is a Canadian documentary *Cat Ladies* by Callan-Jones released in 2009. All of the cat owners in the film were singles; they had up to thirty cats respectively in their households. I think it's noble to adopt ferals, but it may cost a lot to take care of many. It's said that losing a child is the biggest sorrow we can experience; I believe pet owners can guess it as most animals don't live as long as humans. I have cherished memories with my old cat; he had given me enough comforts while staying with me for 17 years.

When we have a pet, I think we can have a chance to observe the entire life of a mammal; I felt life stages of a cat are similar to those of a human. When I got him in 2003, he was vibrant like a child. After he became an adult (1 year old), I noticed that he had spent more time sitting and looking around each year. One day, we realized that he got unusually sluggish and turned out to have blood cancer. Eventually, he could not move at all on the last day of his life. I am sure he had a hard time all the way; I had made a lot of mistakes all along as a first-time cat owner.

Eating meat, which is spending money on killing animals, is a way to be insolvent. A human is a physically weak animal; no one can survive in the Tundra or Amazon jungle alone. Eight billions of weak humans have gathered and built safe communities now; no one has to worry about getting attacked by a tiger on the way to school. We should be happy about it and celebrate. However, I don't think we need to be overly excited. We should not increase our population, expand territories or deplete resources rapidly – **we should not overly exploit the Earth.** When we calm down and benefit others, *Homo sapiens* may last longer than expected.

* * *

I don't know why I wanted a cat so badly in 2003. I was 29 and was in my junior at the University of Buffalo. I failed all the applications to graduate schools before coming to undergraduate again[36] in Buffalo; as a result, I was late for my second undergraduate degree in America after the Korean one. Weirdly, a lot of bad things happened around those years – the darkest era of life (2000-2003). Ironically, the Ferrari photo in the prologue was taken during this time, too. Buffalo was a cold, gray and deteriorating city: a lot of snow, fearfully freezing temps and countless car accidents over the winter. Nothing fancy on the campuses, but tuition[37] was the lowest, which I am still grateful for.

I moved to a new apt in Cheektowaga, NY from the one in front of North Campus since rent was a little cheaper[38]; I thought I needed a change to get out of bad luck by 2003. Yet I have to say that the move was a mistake; the new area was a bad slum, which I didn't realize in the beginning; it was far from the north campus where I studied mostly, too. The north had a lot of decent libraries and most of my classrooms, where I had spent most of my days until I graduated.

Basically, I was alone in the silent but cold apt in the middle of nowhere in 2003. Sometimes, I spoke with my girlfriend[39] over the phone, who studied in Champaign,

---

[36] I had an undergraduate degree from a Korean school.
[37] It was up to $6,000 a semester without scholarship by fall, 2005.
[38] $420 by 2003
[39] My wife now.

IL then.  I remember she said, "I think you are very lonely."  In the worst out of the worst situation, my cat came into my life; I would say **he saved me from getting into more troubles.**

* * *

I have never liked people looking for purebred pets; I hate people buying, selling or smuggling exotic animals; the fact is that a lot of those animals die on the way.  I like people adopting pets from shelters, including SPCA; I am proud I was one of those.  It's a bad idea to buy pets at the mall or from commercial breeders – **none helps animals that way;** breeders don't care about the welfare of animals.  Often, they push some female pets to get pregnant repeatedly.  Besides, customers will definitely overspend on getting pets that way.  I know it costs a lot even after adoptions since I had my cat for 17 years.

By chance, have you heard of pet plastic surgery?  It shows cosmetic procedures include wrinkle removal, tail docking, ear trimming, declawing in felines and debarking in canines; **I heartily oppose declawing since it is extremely painful for cats.** *Personally, giving my cat scratchers had been more than enough for decades.* My girlfriend, who is my wife now, called him Yang; cats are called *"Go-yang-yi"* in Korean, so Yang was the short name from it.  Later on, she made another name for him: Oscar.  I guess she didn't want to go through the hassle of explaining his Korean name whenever visiting hospitals.

Do you know what was the best thing my cat has done for me for almost two decades? **He had helped me stay at home longer.** Then, I had an undesirable habit of driving around for nothing: *Stupid joy rides* on slippery roads during winters. I cannot describe all the minor accidents that happened vainly; a lot of expensive but unpleasant damages happened *unnecessarily* while I was broke, including auto repairs and traffic tickets. It wasn't that I quitted driving around as soon as I adopted the cat – **nonetheless, my pointless joy rides had been less than half suddenly.** Who knows what could have happened if I had stayed outside twice longer? I remember I had slipped off on highways into snow dumps several times; it is probable he might have saved my life.

Unfortunately, Oscar had blood cancer in the end. I especially cherish the memories of the first few months in 2003 and the last months in 2020. He looked OK pretty much throughout his life, but suddenly got worse a month before he passed away. I hated it, but we had to go to the vet to have him euthanized – he couldn't move at all except breathing ultimately, which I assume was typical of cancer patients.

\* \* \*

My parents never had a pet when I grew up.  I remember that I read an article about having cats on a Korean website[40] one day; the writer said he had owned four cats, one by one, for life.  He wrote how much he regretted letting his first cat go only because he had to move to another place.  When he returned to the spot where he abandoned his cat, he actually came out from the basement of an apt nearby and stuck to him; the guy removed him reluctantly since he was about to move away; he said he was still young and thought it was the only way.  When he came back to the place again, he could not find the cat any more.

After ruminating the story for weeks, I visited Erie SPCA[41] in a Buffalo suburb; it was a big, clean facility; a small pet store was inside, too.  The first thing I noticed was a bit of discrimination against a male visitor, which I perceived understandable.  I guess it's reasonable that staff can be suspicious of male adopters; some may be Samaritans, but others can be psychos, too.  Once they handed over animals, there was no practical way they could track them afterwards; they had too many ferals to take care of.

I could not find much hospitality from the shelter volunteers or a cat I felt right with in the first two visits.  They seemed to do the right things apparently.  I could see they did not euthanize animals immediately; they tried to promote adoption as much as they could after

---

[40] Ddanzi.com
[41] Society for the Prevention of Cruelty to Animals.

neutering.  I tried to see my situation logically; I was selfish and didn't do a thing unless it was profitable, which I am not proud of.  I tried to figure out where this strong desire of adoption was from.  In the end, I concluded that this could be the only good thing I do before I die- saving one feral animal. *I was not wrong after spending 17 years with my cat.*  What I didn't expect was that I learned lessons from an animal who I adopted.

After having thought about it weeks more, I returned to the SPCA with my classmate Ricky.  He was a Korean, who was 9 years younger than me; he said he had a cat before and knew a lot of things.  I realized that the attitudes of staff toward me changed to welcoming, instantaneously; I guess that two animal torturers coming to SPCA together are rare.  I still recall that there was a small striped cat trying to clean his face right in front of his cage; the cages were made of silver metal, stacked for three stories.  Oscar was on the second floor right in front of me.  Since they asked me not to touch him, I dangled my keys in front of him; he didn't see me, but saw the keys and tried to touch them.  I always knew that I would have a tabby cat someday.  I said to the staff lady, "I will adopt him."  "Are you sure?"  "Yes."

They processed the adoption promptly; the fee was $65 in 2003.  They put him in a new cardboard box.  Right before they put him in there, he jumped up resisting getting in, but the lady managed to put him in nicely.  Then, they gave me extra stuff:  dry cat food of a

French brand, coupons from vet hospitals, etc.  For some reason, I felt excited as if I won a lottery; I felt like I found a stack of cash on the street – the same feeling when I bought my house.  The same when my daughter was born.  Sang-rok (Ricky) was the Korean guy and we went to PetSmart right after that.  I bought a brand new cat cage which I still have and other stuff: cat litter, a litter box, scoop, extra food, etc.  The cashier lady asked if I just adopted a cat; she said she has two dogs and one cat, which made her busy.  I don't know how I remember everything as if it happened yesterday.

Yang (Oscar) was three-months-old when my wife met him for the first time in Buffalo in 2003; we had countless good memories for the next 17 years.  Later one day, we noticed that he had become notably lagging, so we visited the animal hospital in 2020; the doctor said he had blood cancer and a couple of months to live.  We tried to enjoy the best two months before he passed away.  I brought him out in the garden every night and let him spend hours on the fresh grass during the summer; he couldn't run around any more, and was easily caught by me.  On the last day, I visited a pond for *the first and last time* with him.  My wife, daughter and I brought him to the vet together that afternoon; everyone helped him sleep in peace in my arms.

I bought a shovel from Home Depot and found a warm but quiet spot in a wild area near my home the next day.  He taught me good lessons and spent countless hours snuggling, which helped my blood pressure down.  Finally, he came back to where he was from: He is out of pain and resting in peace now.

## Summary

1. I think it is noble to adopt ferals and take care of them.
2. Some go crazy about spending on pets.
3. Excessive spending is often for humans, and cruel on animals.

# Author's Note

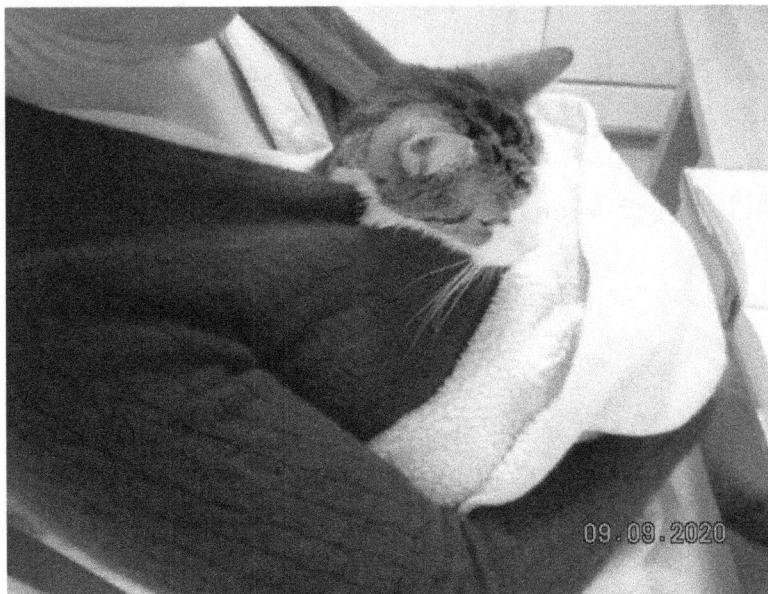

09.09.2020

Congratulations: I truly appreciate you finishing my book until the end. The cat in the photo is Yang (Oscar) who I mentioned many times in Chapter 30 of *UnBrokable\* III*; it was taken only a few days before he passed away. We had so many memories, but he couldn't get over the blood cancer in the end.

I was born and raised in Korea and immigrated to America in my 20s; that was 24 years ago since it's 2023 now. In the beginning, I failed getting accepted to prestigious Ivy league schools although SUNYat Buffalo is a great school. Then I graduated from college with a 2.5 GPA by 2005, so I couldn't get into any graduate school as well. Then I started my own business, but it wasn't very successful for 8 years. Subsequently, my career at the nursing home also didn't work out as I planned even though I won two certificates during the 7 years; now I try to be a writer at the age of 49.

If you believe this book can be helpful to others and have a minute to spare, ***I would truly appreciate a review or rating;*** your help in spreading the word is greatly appreciated. Believe it or not, *I do read all the reviews and use them to improve my writings.* Reviews from readers like you make a huge difference; please let me know what you think. I sincerely wish my best luck to you!

# Acknowledgment

I thank my wife Tsina who has stayed in the living room for the last 10 years. She says it's OK, but it must have been uncomfortable for her.

I also appreciate Amazon who has offered all the platforms to write without charge. I wouldn't have even been a writer if self-publishing was not invented. I thank Google for supporting the writing platform Doc.

Thank you for reading my books.

www.ingramcontent.com/pod-product-compliance
Lightning Source LLC
Chambersburg PA
CBHW021129020426
42331CB00005B/683